Guide to
Field Experiences and
Portfolio Development

Guide to Field Experiences and Portfolio Development

to accompany

Learning to Teach

Sixth Edition

Richard I. Arends

Central Connecticut State University

Higher Education

Boston   Burr Ridge, IL   Dubuque, IA   Madison, WI   New York   San Francisco   St. Louis
Bangkok   Bogotá   Caracas   Kuala Lumpur   Lisbon   London   Madrid   Mexico City
Milan   Montreal   New Delhi   Santiago   Seoul   Singapore   Sydney   Taipei   Toronto

The McGraw·Hill Companies

Guide to Field Experiences and Portfolio Development to accompany
LEARNING TO TEACH, SIXTH EDITION
RICHARD I. ARENDS

Published by McGraw-Hill Higher Education, an imprint of The McGraw-Hill Companies, Inc.,
1221 Avenue of the Americas, New York, NY 10020. Copyright © The McGraw-Hill Companies,
Inc., 2004, 2000, 1998, 1994, 1993, 1991, 1988. All rights reserved.

This book is printed on acid-free paper.

1 2 3 4 5 6 7 8 9 0 QPD QPD 0 9 8 7 6 5 4 3

ISBN 0-07-256459-8

www.mhhe.com

CONTENTS

Introduction. *How to Use This Manual* . . . . **ix**
Nature of Experiential Learning ix
Training the Senses for Experiential Learning xi
The Professional Portfolio xiv
Microteaching or Teaching in Small Groups xv
Reflection and Journaling xvi
Learning from Colleagues and Professional Organizations xvii

Chapter 1. *The Scientific Basis for the Art of Teaching* **1**
Activity 1.1: Assessing My Efforts for Learning to Teach 1
Activity 1.2: Assessing My Teaching Concerns 4
Activity 1.3: Interviewing Teachers about the Scientific
            Basis of the Art of Teaching 5
Activity 1.4: Observing the Three Aspects of Teaching 9
Activity 1.5: Portfolio: My Teaching Platform 10

Chapter 2. *Student Learning in Diverse Classrooms* **11**
Activity 2.1: Assessing My Skills for Promoting Student
            Learning in Diverse Classrooms 11
Activity 2.2: Observing and Interviewing Teachers of Special-Needs
            and Culturally Diverse Students 13
Activity 2.3: Evaluating Curriculum Materials for Bias 16
Activity 2.4: Interviewing a Student from a Different Culture 17
Activity 2.5: Teacher Expectations Questionnaire for Students 18
Activity 2.6: Portfolio: My Understanding of Policies Related
            to Student Learning, Diversity, and Inclusion 19
Activity 2.7: Charting the Characteristics of a School's
            Attendance Boundaries 20

Chapter 3. *Teacher Planning* **23**
Activity 3.1: Assessing My Planning Skills 23
Activity 3.2: Writing Objectives 24
Activity 3.3: Timetabling Techniques 26

Activity 3.4: Observing Lesson Activities and Segments 27
Activity 3.5: Portfolio: Demonstrating My Planning Skills 28

Chapter 4. *Classrooms as Learning Communities* **29**
Activity 4.1: Assessing My Ability to Build Productive Learning Communities . 29
Activity 4.2: Surveying Students about Classroom Life 31
Activity 4.3: Interviewing Teachers about Classroom Goal and
                    Reward Structures 33
Activity 4.4: Portfolio: My Ideas about Positive Classroom
                    Learning Communities 35

Chapter 5. *Classroom Management* **37**
Activity 5.1: Assessing My Classroom Management Skills 37
Activity 5.2: Observing Teachers' Management Behavior 38
Activity 5.3: Observing Students' Influence on
                    Academic Tasks 40
Activity 5.4: Interviewing Teachers about Rules and Procedures 41
Activity 5.5: Observing Management Practices during Unstable Periods 44
Activity 5.6: Observing Teacher Responses to Student Misbehavior 46
Activity 5.7: Portfolio: My Classroom Management Platform 48

Chapter 6. *Assessment and Evaluation* **49**
Activity 6.1: Assessing My Assessment and Evaluation Skills 49
Activity 6.2: Interviewing Teachers about Their Evaluation and
                    Grading Procedures 50
Activity 6.3: Constructing a Test Blueprint 52
Activity 6.4: Analyzing Teacher-Made Tests 53
Activity 6.5: Reflecting on the Future of Assessment
                    and Evaluation 54
Activity 6.6: Portfolio: Demonstrating My Skill for
                    Performance Assessment 55

Chapter 7. *Presentation* **57**
Activity 7.1: Assessing My Presentation Skills 57
Activity 7.2: Lesson Plan for Presentation 58
Activity 7.3: Observing a Presentation in Microteaching
                    or Classrooms 60
Activity 7.4: Observing Teacher Clarity 62
Activity 7.5: Portfolio: Creating My Own Presentation Lesson

Using an Advance Organizer 63

Chapter 8. *Direct Instruction* **65**
Activity 8.1: Assessing My Skills for Using the Direct Instruction Model 65
Activity 8.2: Lesson Plan Format for a Direct Instruction Model Lesson 66
Activity 8.3: Observing Direct Instruction in Microteaching or Classrooms . . 68
Activity 8.4: Observing Teacher Use of Practice 69
Activity 8.5: Portfolio: Showing My Use of Task Analysis
              and Demonstration 71

Chapter 9. *Concept Teaching* **73**
Activity 9.1: Assessing My Skills for Concept Teaching 73
Activity 9.2: Observing a Concept Attainment Lesson in
              Microteaching or Classrooms 75
Activity 9.3: Concept Analysis 77
Activity 9.4: Analyzing Curriculum Guides for
              Concept Lessons 78
Activity 9.5: Portfolio: Demonstrating My Webbing Skills 79

Chapter 10. *Cooperative Learning* **81**
Activity 10.1: Assessing My Skills for Using Cooperative Learning 81
Activity 10.2: Observing Cooperative Learning in Microteaching
               or Classrooms 82
Activity 10.3: Observing Small-Group Interaction 84
Activity 10.4: Observing Transitions and Group Management 85
Activity 10.5: Visiting the School's Library, Media Center,
               and/or Computer Laboratory 86
Activity 10.6: Portfolio: Creating Your Own Lesson for
               Teaching Social Skills 88

Chapter 11. *Problem-Based Learning* **89**
Activity 11.1: Assessing My Skills for Problem-Based Learning 89
Activity 11.2: Lesson Plan Format for Problem Instruction Lesson 90
Activity 11.3: Observing Problem-Based Learning in Microteaching
               or Classrooms 92
Activity 11.4: Interviewing Teachers about Their Use of
               Problem-Based Learning 94
Activity 11.5: Portfolio: Designing and Illustrating
               Problem Situations 95

Chapter 12. *Classroom Discussion* **97**
   Activity 12.1: Assessing My Discussion and Discourse Skills 97
   Activity 12.2: Observing Discussion in Microteaching
                  or Classrooms 98
   Activity 12.3: Observing Student Participation in Discussion 100
   Activity 12.4: Observing Teacher Use of Questions
                  and Wait-Time 101
   Activity 12.5: Portfolio: Demonstrating Your Executive Control
                  of Questioning 103

Chapter 13. *School Leadership and Collaboration* **105**
   Activity 13.1: Assessing My Workplace Skills 105
   Activity 13.2: Diagnosing the School's Ability to Meet Personal Needs 106
   Activity 13.3: Interviewing Teachers about Role Conflict 109
   Activity 13.4: Interviewing Teachers about Involving Parents 110
   Activity 13.5: Portfolio: My Platform on Effective Schooling 112

Notes *113*

INTRODUCTION

HOW TO USE THIS MANUAL

Learning to teach is a long-term journey. It takes purposeful action and careful reflection fueled by a desire for excellence; it requires an attitude that learning to teach is a lifelong process in which individuals gradually discover their own style through reflection and critical inquiry into one's own teaching. This *Field Experience and Portfolio Manual* has been written to help you start your journey. It contains a variety of activities for you to use, including visiting classrooms, observing teachers or videos, interviewing teachers or students, talking to peers, reflecting with colleagues, and developing sample artifacts for your portfolio, such as journal entries, videotapes, or reflective essays.

As you begin your journey, you will find that there are some aspects of teaching that can be learned in a college classroom; others can be learned by studying what researchers and experienced teachers have to say about the topic. However, many of the most important features of the art of professional practice can be learned only through experience. This manual describes how you can learn from your experiences while you are still in your teacher preparation program and beginning years of your career. It reinforces a point of view described in Chapter 1: Learning to teach is a lifelong process, and effective teachers become that way by having a learning agenda for lifelong growth coupled with careful analysis and reflection that produces this growth. Three facets of learning from experience are described here: the nature of experiential learning, developing the receptive skills—listening and observing—that promote learning from experience, and critical review and reflection.

Nature of Experiential Learning

Everyone learns from experience and knows that experience is a basis for new ideas and behavior. For example, you probably learned to ride your first bicycle by riding one, and you learned about being a sister or brother by being one. Experience provides insights, understandings, and techniques that are difficult to describe to anyone who has not had similar experiences. The same is true for teaching.

Experiential learning differs from much of the learning that people are exposed to as students. Instead of starting with a set of academic principles or rules, in experiential learning learners start with concrete experiences or activities and then, by observing their own behavior and that of others, formulate concepts and principles that can be applied to new situations. This perspective is illustrated in Figure 1.

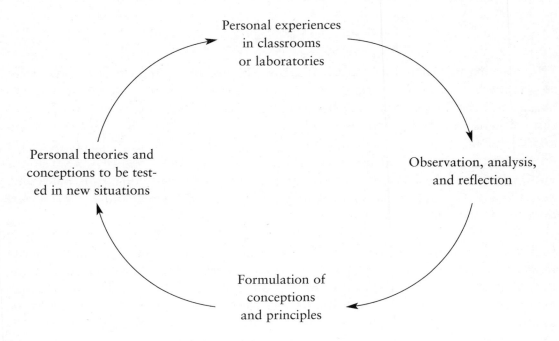

FIGURE 1. *Cyclical Nature of Experiential Learning*

Dewey (1938) suggested that to learn from experience is to make a backward-forward connection between what we do to things and what we learn from these things and experiences. Johnson and Johnson (1998) provided a more detailed explanation:

> Experiential learning is based upon three assumptions: that you learn best when you are personally involved in the learning experience, that knowledge has to be discovered by yourself if it is to mean anything to you or make a difference in your behavior, and that a commitment to learning is highest when you are free to set your own learning goals and actively pursue them within a given framework. Experiential learning is a process of making generalizations and conclusions about your own direct experiences. It emphasizes directly experiencing what you are studying, building your own commitment to learn, and your being partly responsible for organizing the conclusions drawn from your experiences (p. 7).

The theory behind experiential learning is, in many ways, very similar to the principles on which the constructivist perspective about learning rest. As described in Chapter 1, learning from a constructivist perspective is not viewed as passively receiving information from someone else, but instead as actively engaging in relevant experiences and having opportunities for dialogue and reflection. This type of learning is especially useful in complex learning situations such as teaching, which can never be completely described to the beginner. It is also useful for applying many of the skills and guidelines described in *Learning to Teach*.

Experience alone, however, is not sufficient. For best results, the learner must be willing to depend less upon the teacher than in other types of learning. The learner must have a set of learning skills, that is, must be able to observe and reflect on experiences in order to conceptualize from them. The following sections describe some of these skills in more detail.

Training the Senses for Experiential Learning

People learn from experience primarily through their senses. Two are of particular importance for learning to teach: listening critically and observing keenly. These come together through reflective thinking and analysis.

Listening.   Learning to listen carefully and pick up subtle cues from experienced, expert teachers is one important skill for those learning to teach. On the surface, listening appears simple but, in fact, it is a rather complex, sophisticated process. It has been observed that most people strike one of three listening postures when they hear new information or are experiencing a new environment for the first time.

The first listening posture, and by far the most common, is to listen for information that *confirms* what you already know. Although such information can be important, such a posture is obviously limiting. You may think that a person who says things you already believe is pretty smart, but you don't really learn much from what you hear. If your posture is only to listen for supporting comments, you may actively distort the meanings of what others say.

The second listening posture, one that seems fairly rare, is to *seek answers* to honest questions. When you recognize a discrepancy or dilemma for which you personally need an answer, you can formulate honest questions about it. Often the need for certainty in our lives makes us uncomfortable with honest questions, so we either discredit the questions or seek only superficial answers. If, however, you seek answers to honest questions, you are likely to hear more and differently than those who do not. Honest questions that are not simply critical doubting give direction to listening and new meanings to information. However, questions also have a limiting effect. They tend to restrict your attention to information that seems relevant to your questions, a process referred to as selective perception. Also, questions invite certain interpretations of information to the exclusion of other possibilities. They tend to create a "set" for understanding.

The third listening posture, which is very rare, involves being open to information as a means of creating new insights and perspectives. How many people saw apples fall before Newton conceived the laws of gravity? In a world of continuous, accelerating change and awesome technologies, it is essential that we listen for new understandings and new ways to comprehend our experience. Paradoxically, we simultaneously sense that our ways of experiencing are limited yet believe that the basis for all human understanding already lies within our experiences.

Observing.   Although classroom observation is one of the most frequently used ways to learn about teaching, observation alone is insufficient and can, in fact, lead to incorrect conclusions. This is true for several reasons, two of which are most important. First, when you go into a classroom to observe, you take with you a host of anxieties and biases from past experiences; and, second, life in classrooms is a series of rapidly moving, complex events. Each of these problems is described in more detail in the sections that follow.

BIAS AND ANXIETY.   You are all aware of many instances in everyday life in which bias and anxiety distort people's perceptions. Note the number of times that victims or eyewitnesses of criminal acts are unable to give investigators a detailed or complete description of the event, just moments after it occurred. Or think of the times that the wrong person is picked out of a police lineup. Think also of the times that you have heard two friends tell you about what they saw on a vacation they took together and the wide discrepancies in their reports.

Being an eyewitness to classroom events is no different from witnessing other events, except it may be a bit more complicated. Every person in the process of learning to teach has biases that influence what he or she attends to while observing classrooms. These may involve concepts of good teaching or, perhaps, values about what is appropriate behavior for children and young adults. They may be attitudes about classroom life carried over from early experiences as a student—a sense of boredom and withdrawal associated with a grammar lesson, or antipathy to a teacher with a gruff voice. The important point is that these concepts, values, attitudes, and past experiences inevitably influence what an observer perceives and learns from classroom observation.

Anxiety is another important influence, particularly for beginning teachers. When people are nervous and anxious in a situation, their vision and perceptual fields tend to narrow, and they miss much that they normally would attend to. When beginning teachers are observers in someone else's classroom, it is natural for them to be unsure and to worry, "Are we intruding on the teacher's lesson? Why are the children looking at us?" Similarly, initial teaching situations are stressful, anxiety producing, uncomfortable. A normal reaction is to distort what is observed and, many times, to ignore threatening information.

CLASSROOM COMPLEXITY.   Finally, it is difficult to observe accurately in classrooms because events move rapidly and the total classroom environment is complex. Many have observed that teachers have literally thousands of independent interactions daily with students—more interactions with clients than occur in any other occupation except perhaps air traffic controlling. Classrooms with teacher aides and where teachers have several small groups working simultaneously present even more rapid movement and complexity.

GUIDELINES FOR OBSERVING IN CLASSROOMS.   Several steps can be taken to overcome bias in observation and to reduce the complexity of classroom life. If followed, they can make observations more accurate and more valuable as learning experiences. Several guidelines are offered below that have been found useful by beginning teachers as well as researchers (see, for example, Good & Brophy, 1999).

Guideline 1: Become Aware of One's Own Values, Attitudes, and Conceptual Blinders

People never become completely aware of their attitudes and prejudices, just as they are never completely aware of the sources of daily fears and anxieties. However, setting aside time now and then for self-reflection and introspection heightens awareness.

Guideline 2: Make Careful Arrangements with Teachers before Observations

Careful arrangements before a visit will relieve some of the anxiety associated with observations in a strange classroom. A talk with the teacher, either in person or over the phone, a few days before a visit will help clarify expectations about what you want to accomplish as an observer and about how the teacher wants you to behave during the visit. Arrangements can be made about where you should sit, how you are to be introduced to the class, and so on.

Guideline 3: Reduce Complexity by Focusing Observations

Even the most experienced observers cannot see everything going on in a classroom, so they focus on particular events or behaviors. This is particularly important for the beginner. One does this by either observing a few of the actors in the classroom—four or five students rather than the whole class—or watching for a few behaviors at a time, such as the way students respond to a teacher's questions or praise. The learning aid sections of this book provide several recommendations for focusing classroom observations by reducing complexity.

Guideline 4: Attend Mainly to Observable Behaviors

A very common cause of distortion in what a person sees is that too often the observer tries to interpret motives from behavior instead of just observing it. Take, for example, the following written notes from an observation.

"The teacher spoke in a loud voice and frowned."

"The teacher was angry with the children."

The first is an example of what the observer actually saw. The second is an interpretation of the teacher's feelings. Observers should concentrate on observable behavior, as in the first example.

Guideline 5: Remain Unobtrusive during Observations

Harry Walcott, a noted educational anthropologist, once wrote that when he was observing people in any social setting he "keeps his eyes on his paper and his pencil going all the time." This is important advice for classroom observers. A note taken once in a while cues teachers and students about what the observer is looking for. Making eye contact with students in class increases the chances of their wanting to interact with the observer, thus interrupting the observer's concentration and perhaps the teacher's lesson.

Guideline 6: Extend a Thank-You to the Teacher and to the Students (If Appropriate) after Your Observation

Observers are guests in classrooms. A thank-you is required just as it would be to a friend at whose home you spent a weekend.

The Professional Portfolio

The encouragement of educators to develop professional portfolios has accelerated in the past several years as the importance of reflective problem solving and critical inquiry has increased. Assembling a portfolio develops reflective thinking, decision making, and evaluation skills, and as a learning device it has been picked up by teacher educators for its potential for promotion reflective thinking and inquiry.

A portfolio is a collection of ideas, artifacts, and products that provides an authentic means for teachers to represent their views on teaching, their work, and their students' work. Portfolios are not just something you do one time; they are useful for keeping a record of professional growth over a lifetime of learning to teach. They are particularly useful for displaying your work when interviewing for a teaching position. Many teacher education programs require teacher candidates to build a portfolio early in their program so it can evolve and mature as the candidate grows and changes. Some states also require portfolios as part of the evaluation process for beginning teachers.

At the end of each chapter of *Learning to Teach,* you will find a feature called "Portfolio and Field Experience Activities." This feature has been designed to help you reflect on the important ideas covered in the chapter and to develop artifacts that can be placed in your portfolio.

Items most teachers put in their portfolios include reflective essays showing how they think about teaching and learning, artifacts such as sample units of work or lesson plans, and samples of their students' work, particularly work that shows how the teacher has impacted student learning. Some teachers also include photos and videos showing classroom teaching and student interaction.

There is no particular format to follow in a portfolio. However, the portfolio, like all work, should be neat, organized, and creative. Most important, the portfolio should represent you. Many of you will choose to use *FolioLive*, an online portfolio tool to create an electronic portfolio in three easy steps: (1) use a template to create a home page; (2) choose to create a custom framework or frameworks to structure your portfolio; and (3) add the artifacts to build your portfolio. Go to www.foliolive.com to learn more about this product.

Microteaching or Teaching in Small Groups

Listening and observing in classrooms is one form of experience. Another is microteaching: actual practice in scaled-down situations. In microteaching, you arrange to teach a brief lesson to a small group of students in an actual classroom, or you teach a short lesson to your peers. Microteaching is an invaluable experiential process for learning to teach and for helping you begin to consolidate your teaching knowledge and skill. It is an effective means of offering practice and feedback and an activity that is valued very highly by beginning teachers who participate in it. As with any endeavor, microteaching requires planning and organizing to ensure its success. The following guidelines are offered to assist you in your planning for microteaching, whether as a part of your teacher education program or as something you decide to arrange on your own.

1. *Microteaching requires a small-group setup.* Microteaching is best accomplished with groups of six to eight students or peers. If using peers, each group needs a facilitator. This can be one of your peers, a professor, or a clinical teacher. The role of the facilitator is to ensure that all microteachers have adequate time to give their lesson and to receive feedback.

2. *Microteaching with peers requires a large chunk of time.* Each microteacher needs enough time to adequately present a brief lesson and receive feedback on it. Generally, lesson presentations run about 10 to 12 minutes, followed by 5 to 10 minutes of feedback from peers or students and the facilitator. This means that 2 to 3 hours must be set aside for each microteaching lesson if six to ten persons are involved. In actual classrooms, with just one person microteaching, less time is required.

3. *Special equipment is needed.* Ideally a microteaching lab should be available, and many colleges and universities have this type of facility. The lab should be outfitted with a video camera and recording equipment and should contain the audiovisual supplies usually found in classrooms (for example, overhead projector and screen, chalkboard, chalk, and erasers) for use by students in their presentations. Microteachers need to bring a blank tape with them so their lessons can be recorded for later use. In a laboratory where microteaching is being done with peers, the job of recording each lesson can be rotated. In a real classroom, the teacher or one of the students can be asked to assist with recording the lesson.

   If a special room set aside for microteaching cannot be arranged, a roll-around video recording system or camcorder can be used. With a roll-around, the camera and recorder system are lodged on a cart and wheeled to rooms where microteaching sections are to be held. If video is not at all feasible, audio recording can be used as a last resort.

4. *Feedback is a vital element of microteaching.* Whether you are microteaching with real students or peers, feedback on the lesson is critical. Feedback should be specific and should include both recognition for good performance and constructive criticism. Comments such as, "I liked how you projected enthusiasm with all your gesturing," or "It would have been easier to understand your advance organizer if you had provided a visual aid" are much more useful than a general, "I enjoyed your lesson." If real students are being asked to provide feedback, they will need to be given explicit directions on how to provide feedback. Chapter 8 contains information on how to give feedback.

   If you are using microteaching to practice one of the models described in Chapters 7–12 in *Learning to Teach*, it will be helpful to use the appropriate observation instruments provided in this manual. Students or your peers can fill out the instrument as they follow the lesson and recall the particulars during the feedback phase, and you will have something concrete to take away and reflect upon.

5. *Remember analysis and reflection.* A microteaching practice session will be of most value if you watch the videotape of your lesson and reflect on the feedback you received. Sometimes a short written critique about how the lesson went, incorporating the feedback you received, is a good learning device.

Reflection and Journaling

Through reflection, experiences become more valuable. It is when teachers start to conceptualize and formulate their own rules and principles that they start to build personal theories to guide their teaching practice and serve as springboards for new discoveries.

But how does one begin reflecting? Although reflective thinking is not a haphazard trial-and-error process, neither can it be scheduled to happen every morning at 9:15 A.M., as jogging can be.

One of the most productive ways to foster reflective thinking is by using a journal. Here is advice to beginning teachers provided by Frank Lyman (personal correspondence, no date) a teacher-educator at the University of Maryland, about how to approach the process of reflection:

> A person learns by experience. However, for the fastest, most advanced learning to take place, disciplined reflection is necessary. Experience is not the best teacher; reflection, or analysis, is. There are many ways to reflect on experience and it is helpful to try out several. During student teaching, you will master one way and be invited to invent others. The journaling strategy is the prescribed way. Use it four times a week. For the fifth entry use any format to probe an issue related to curriculum/instruction/school climate. If you can invent an effective strategy for analyzing a teaching/learning event, show me.

Learning from Colleagues and Professional Organizations

An additional source of experiential learning for beginning teachers is the learning that comes from interaction with colleagues and at professional meetings. Unfortunately, many beginning teachers do not seem to have good professional networks and do not regularly attend professional meetings. It is important for beginning teachers to set goals for themselves early in their careers that will help guide professional experiences and growth. In the Online Learning Center is a list of the names and addresses of several professional organizations that have meetings nationally and locally where teachers can learn about research and interact with colleagues. An example of such a professional organization is the Association for Supervision and Curriculum Development (ASCD). This organization publishes a monthly journal, *Educational Leadership,* that contains many interpretive articles on research. The organization also has local units in every state that produce newsletters and hold regular meetings of interest to teachers. Phi Delta Kappa also provides similar services to teachers, as do the National Education Association, the American Federation of Teachers, and many subject-specialty associations. A beginning teacher who wants to grow will become a member of some of these associations and will build a network of colleagues interested in improving their teaching by keeping abreast of the latest research and practices.

CHAPTER 1

THE SCIENTIFIC BASIS FOR THE ART OF TEACHING

Activity 1.1   Assessing My Efforts for Learning to Teach
Activity 1.2   Assessing My Teaching Concerns
Activity 1.3   Interviewing Teachers about the Scientific Basis of the Art of Teaching
Activity 1.4   Observing the Three Aspects of Teaching
Activity 1.5   Portfolio: My Teaching Platform

Activity 1.1: Assessing My Efforts for Learning to Teach

Purpose: One of the most important goals of *Learning to Teach* is to inspire your continuing efforts at professional development. This activity will help you to gain an overall impression of your efforts to pursue the attributes of effective teaching described in Chapter 1 and to reflect on and plan for the next steps in your own professional growth.

Directions: Circle the response that best corresponds to your level of agreement with the statement, then list the relevant activities under each category. Use the information to pinpoint gaps in your professional development activities.

1. I am actively engaged in developing personal dispositions toward teaching in ways that will allow me to develop authentic relationships with students and work toward socially just classrooms. (*Circle one.*)

   Agree strongly   Agree   Neither agree nor disagree   Disagree   Disagree strongly

   Dispositions I feel I have developed quite fully:

   _____

   _____

   Dispositions I need to work on:

   _____

   _____

   _____

2. I am actively engaged in developing my command of the knowledge base for teaching. (*Circle one.*)

Agree strongly   Agree   Neither agree nor disagree   Disagree   Disagree strongly

Topics I feel comfortable with   Topics I am currently working on   Topics I will work on next

_____   _____   _____

_____   _____   _____

_____   _____   _____

_____   _____   _____

3. I am actively engaged in reflecting on myself as a teacher and in problem solving around educational issues. (*Circle one.*)

Agree strongly   Agree   Neither agree nor disagree   Disagree   Disagree strongly

Ways I currently reflect on and solve problems about teaching:

_____

_____

_____

New ways I want to learn to help me reflect on and solve problems about teaching:

_____

_____

_____

4. I am actively engaged in expanding my repertoire of teaching practices. (*Circle one.*)

Agree strongly   Agree   Neither agree nor disagree   Disagree   Disagree strongly

Practices I know   Practices I am currently learning   Practices I will study next

_____   _____   _____

_____   _____   _____

_____   _____   _____

_____   _____   _____

5. I am actively engaged in the lifelong process of learning to teach. (*Circle one.*)

Agree strongly   Agree   Neither agree nor disagree   Disagree   Disagree strongly

Past actions I have taken to help me learn about teaching:

_____

_____

_____

Actions I am currently taking to help me learn about teaching:

_____

_____

_____

Actions I plan to take in the future to help me continue to learn about teaching:

_____

_____

_____

Activity 1.2: Assessing My Teaching Concerns

Purpose: Learning to teach is a developmental process—people progress through stages—and awareness of the stage you're in can facilitate this process. This activity will help you develop awareness of your level of concern about teaching.

Directions: Read each statement, then ask yourself: When I think about my teaching, how much am I concerned about this?

1 Not concerned	4 Very concerned
2 A little concerned	5 Extremely concerned
3 Moderately concerned	

Being concerned about something is not the same as thinking it is important. Being concerned means you think about it frequently and would like to do something about it personally. Thus, you can be concerned about problems or opportunities, current or anticipated issues, and so on. For each issue, circle the number that best corresponds to your level of concern.

1. Lack instruction materials	1	2	3	4	5
2. Feel under pressure too much of the time	1	2	3	4	5
3. Do well when a supervisor is present	1	2	3	4	5
4. Meet the needs of different kinds of students	1	2	3	4	5
5. Have too many noninstructional duties	1	2	3	4	5
6. Diagnose student learning problems	1	2	3	4	5
7. Feel more adequate as a teacher	1	2	3	4	5
8. Challenge unmotivated students	1	2	3	4	5
9. Am accepted and respected by professional persons	1	2	3	4	5
10. Work with too many students each day	1	2	3	4	5
11. Guide students toward intellectual growth	1	2	3	4	5
12. Give each student what he or she needs	1	2	3	4	5
13. Get a favorable evaluation of my teaching	1	2	3	4	5
14. Accept the routine and inflexibility of teaching	1	2	3	4	5
15. Maintain the appropriate degree of class control	1	2	3	4	5

Analysis and Reflection: One way to reflect is to arrange your concerns in order of importance and compare them with those of others. You may think of other ways to help you reflect on your teaching concerns. In addition, you may want to keep a log for 5 days, each day writing a brief paragraph about the concerns you have experienced about teaching or your anticipation of teaching (Based on Fuller, 1969).

Activity 1.3: Interviewing Teachers about the Scientific Basis of the Art of Teaching

Purpose: Teaching is both science and art. This activity will help you to uncover an experienced teacher's perceptions about the scientific basis of the art of teaching and to develop your own appreciation of teaching as art and science.

Directions: Use the following questions to guide you as you interview a teacher about his or her understanding and application of the scientific basis of the art of teaching. (Note: Many experienced teachers may not be aware of the research base and yet may be using best practice. Some effective teaching research is based on what excellent experienced teachers do.)

1. To what extent has the way you plan your teaching been influenced by: (*Estimate the percentage contribution of each.*)
   _____ research on planning
   _____ your own experience and intuition
   _____ other (please specify) _____

2. Can you give an example of a planning principle you have learned from each source?
   research: _____
   experience: _____
   other: _____

3. Do you find you sometimes need to modify these principles in practice? If so, in what way(s)?

   _____

   _____

   _____

4. To what extent has the way you allocate resources like time and space in your classroom been influenced by: (*Estimate the percentage contribution of each.*)
   _____ research on allocating time and space
   _____ your own experience and intuition
   _____ other (*please specify*) _____

5. Can you give an example of a principle of allocating resources that you have learned from each source?
   research: _____
   experience: _____
   other: _____

6. Do you find you sometimes need to modify these principles in practice? If so, in what way(s)?

   _____

   _____

   _____

7. To what extent has the way you organize your classroom to create a productive classroom community been influenced by: (*Estimate the percentage contribution of each.*)
   _____ research
   _____ your own experience and intuition
   _____ other (*please specify*) _____

8. Can you give an example of a principle underlying the creation of productive classroom community you have learned from each source?
   research: _____
   experience: _____
   other: _____

9. Do you find you sometimes need to modify these principles in practice? If so, in what way(s)?

   _____

   _____

   _____

10. To what extent has the way you manage your classroom been influenced by: (*Estimate the percentage contribution of each.*)
    _____ research
    _____ your own experience and intuition
    _____ other (*please specify*) _____

11. Can you give an example of a classroom management principle that you have learned from each source?
   research: _____
   experience: _____
   other: _____

12. Do you find you sometimes need to modify these principles in practice? If so, in what way(s)?

   _____

   _____

   _____

13. To what extent are the teaching strategies you use influenced by: (*Estimate the percentage contribution of each.*)
   _____ research
   _____ your own experience and intuition
   _____ other (*please specify*) _____

14. Can you give an example of a teaching strategy that you have learned from each source?
   research: _____
   experience: _____
   other: _____

15. Do you find you sometimes need to modify these strategies in practice? If so, in what way(s)?

   _____

   _____

   _____

16. To what extent is the way you work with other adults in the school influenced by: (*Estimate the percentage contribution of each.*)
   _____ research
   _____ your own experience and intuition
   _____ other (*please specify*) _____

17. Can you give examples of principles underlying work with parents that you have learned from each source?

    research: _____

    experience: _____

    other: _____

18. Do you find you sometimes need to modify these principles in practice? If so, in what way(s)?

    _____

    _____

    _____

Analysis and Reflection: Are there any patterns to where this teacher obtains ideas or principles for teaching? Are there any patterns to how this teacher modifies these ideas or principles in practice? Write a paragraph about any patterns you perceive and their relevance to your own teaching.

Activity 1.4: Observing the Three Aspects of Teaching

Purpose: Teaching is a complex, multifaceted activity. This activity will help sensitize you to the multiple aspects of a teacher's work.

Directions: Shadow a teacher for at least half a day. Make sure you have a chance to observe him or her either before school starts or after class is let out. Make a "tick" whenever you see the teacher perform one of the listed activities. At the same time, estimate the amount of time the teacher spends on that activity, and jot down any other observations you make. Perhaps certain activities tend to occur at certain times, a particular emotional tone is evident, or several activities occur simultaneously. Make note of anything you think will help you refine your understanding of the three aspects of teaching.

Aspect	Observed	Time	Comments
Leadership			
Planning	_____	_____	_____
Allocating time and space	_____	_____	_____
Organizing learning communities	_____	_____	_____
Managing the classroom	_____	_____	_____
Assessing or evaluating	_____	_____	_____
Interaction			
Using the presentation model	_____	_____	_____
Using the direct instruction model	_____	_____	_____
Using the cooperative learning model	_____	_____	_____
Using problem-based learning	_____	_____	_____
Using concept teaching models	_____	_____	_____
Using discussion	_____	_____	_____
Using other strategies (*specify*)	_____	_____	_____
Organization			
Interacting with other adults to carry out the work of the school	_____	_____	_____
Working alone on nonclassroom tasks	_____	_____	_____
Working toward school improvement	_____	_____	_____
Working with parents	_____	_____	_____

Analysis and Reflection   Tally up the number of ticks for each category, and add the amount of time spent on each category. What did this teacher spend the most time doing? What did he or she do most often? How much time is spent on average on any one episode within a category? (Divide time spent by number of ticks.) Does this seem to be the most productive allocation of the teacher's time? Why or why not?

Activity 1.5: Portfolio: My Teaching Platform

Purpose: This first portfolio activity was designed to help you describe your current thinking about teaching and learning by creating a **teaching platform.**

Directions: Create a teaching platform by doing the following:

STEP 1:   Write a two- or three-page paper that describes your platform for teaching and learning. This platform should represent your thinking at this point in time about how learning occurs and the implications this has for teaching practices. Your platform should be supported by clear and specific "planks" that include the beliefs and values that guide the way you would construct your classroom and perform your teaching.

Think about the platform as your overall conception about teaching and learning, and the planks as your more specific beliefs and values. An example of a plank might be that "learning is an active process wherein knowledge is socially constructed."

STEP 2:   Your platform should be started now, preferably early in the semester. Revise it weekly as you study and learn more about all aspects of teaching and learning to teach.

STEP 3:   You may also wish to use your platform as a device to organize other aspects of your portfolio. For instance, you might illustrate your beliefs with photographs, videos, papers, lesson plans, and examples of student work.

SOURCE: The ideas in this activity are adapted from work done by Dr. Paulette Lemma and her colleagues in the Elementary Education Program at Connecticut State University.

CHAPTER 2

STUDENT LEARNING IN DIVERSE CLASSROOMS

Activity 2.1   Assessing My Skills for Promoting Student Learning in Diverse Classrooms
Activity 2.2   Observing and Interviewing Teachers of Special-Needs and Culturally Diverse Students
Activity 2.3   Evaluating Curriculum Materials for Bias
Activity 2.4   Interviewing a Student from a Different Culture
Activity 2.5   Teacher Expectations Questionnaire for Students
Activity 2.6   Portfolio: My Understanding of Policies Related to Student Learning, Diversity, and Inclusion
Activity 2.7   Charting the Characteristics of a School's Attendance Boundaries

Activity 2.1: Assessing My Skills for Promoting Student Learning in Diverse Classrooms

Purpose: This aid is designed to help you assess your abilities in developing a classroom and teaching practices where all children will learn. Use it to assist in planning your own professional development.

Directions: Check the level of effectiveness you believe you have attained in each of the following areas.

Understanding or Skill	Level of Understanding or Skill		
	High	Medium	Low
My understanding of:			
The importance of equity	_____	_____	_____
The effects of differential treatments	_____	_____	_____
Student abilities and learning styles	_____	_____	_____
Student exceptionalities	_____	_____	_____
Culture, race, and ethnicity	_____	_____	_____
Culturally diverse classrooms	_____	_____	_____
Multicultural education	_____	_____	_____
Language diversity	_____	_____	_____
Gender differences	_____	_____	_____
Social class differences	_____	_____	_____
My ability to:			
Treat students fairly	_____	_____	_____
Show respect for all students	_____	_____	_____
Work with students with disabilities	_____	_____	_____
Work with gifted students	_____	_____	_____
Work with racially and culturally diverse students	_____	_____	_____
Work with language-diverse students	_____	_____	_____
Work with gender differences			
Work with low-SES students	_____	_____	_____
Plan and implement lessons where all students will learn	_____	_____	_____
Use culturally relevant pedagogy	_____	_____	_____

Analysis and Reflection: What are your strengths for promoting student learning in diverse classroom? What are your weaknesses? Write a reflective essay and action plan for your portfolio describing your view of promoting student learning in diverse classrooms and how you will address your own professional growth in this area.

Activity 2.2: Observing and Interviewing Teachers of Special-Needs and Culturally Diverse Students

Purpose: It's relatively simple to vow to treat all children equitably, but it's sometimes difficult to put such ideals into practice. This activity will help you learn how experienced teachers actually accomplish the goal of fair and effective treatment of exceptional, limited-English, and culturally diverse students.

Directions: First observe, then interview, a teacher about how he or she manages a classroom with special-needs and diverse children, using the observation and interview form below as a guide. Observe and note the following:

1. How has the teacher arranged the furniture in the room?

   _____

   _____

   _____

2. What has the teacher placed on the walls? Are they brightly and busily decorated or more subdued? Are rules, procedures, or other cues posted?

   _____

   _____

   _____

3. Note the teacher's use of time. How much time is devoted, on average, to each lesson segment? Do students move around much between lesson segments? How much time does the teacher provide for transitions?

   _____

   _____

   _____

4. How has the teacher grouped students for instruction? Whole class? Individual? Small groups? Do the students stay in the same grouping pattern, or do they change from one arrangement to another?

   _____

   _____

   _____

5. What rules and procedures do students observe in this classroom?

_____

_____

_____

6. Note peer interaction. Tally the number of positive and negative statements students make to each other.

_____

_____

_____

7. What teaching strategy is the teacher using?

_____

_____

Now that you've observed the class, use the questions below to guide an interview with the teacher.

8. What is your strategy for dealing with the wide range of academic ability, diverse language ability, and cultural diversity in your classroom?

_____

_____

_____

9. How did you come to this strategy? Where did you get your ideas? What else have you tried, and how successful was it?

_____

_____

_____

10. How have you helped special-needs students be accepted by other children?

_____

_____

_____

11. Do you have pull-out programs (a program in which a child with special needs is "pulled out" of his or her regular classroom for instruction by a special teacher) in your school? If so, how do you work around learning-disabled students going in and out? Gifted and talented students? Limited-English students?

_____

_____

_____

Analysis and Reflection: Based on what you have read, observed, and discussed with teachers, briefly outline your own plan for how you will accommodate special-needs children in your own class. What obstacles are you likely to run into in implementing your plan? How might you circumvent them?

Activity 2.3: Evaluating Curriculum Materials for Bias

Purpose: The purpose of this activity is to systematically assess bias in textbooks and other learning materials.

Directions: Select an elementary or secondary school textbook to evaluate, either from a school in which you are doing fieldwork or from the university curriculum library. Read it, paying special attention to the content, examples, and visual material in it. Then fill out the charts here; write a "Y" for "yes" in the appropriate blank if the book exhibits that particular form of bias for that particular group.

1. Look at the *content* of the book—the information conveyed. Are any of these forms of bias present: stereotype, imbalance, invisibility, unreality, linguistic, fragmentation?
   Race/ethnicity: _____
   Gender: _____
   Low-SES: _____
   Special needs: _____

2. Look at the *examples* used to elaborate on and clarify the content. Are any of these forms of bias present: stereotype, imbalance, invisibility, unreality, linguistic, fragmentation?
   Race/ethnicity: _____
   Gender: _____
   Low-SES: _____
   Special needs: _____

3. Look at the *visuals* used to illustrate the content. Are any of these forms of bias present: stereotype, imbalance, invisibility, unreality, linguistic, fragmentation?
   Race/ethnicity: _____
   Gender: _____
   Low-SES: _____
   Special needs: _____

Analysis and Reflection: Does the book contain bias? Would you use it in your own classroom? Why or why not? If you did use it, how would you raise the issue of bias with your students? Alternatively, how would you supplement the text to provide a bias-free curriculum?

Activity 2.4: Interviewing a Student from a Different Culture

Purpose: Part of developing knowledge and skill in teaching multiculturally is learning about different cultures, especially about how people from different cultures fare in schools. You can use this activity to learn more about culturally diverse students.

Directions: Use the questions below to guide an interview with a student from a subculture.

1. What are the similarities you've noticed between your own culture and the mainstream culture?

   _____

   _____

2. What are some of the differences you've noticed between your culture and the mainstream culture?

   _____

   _____

3. What do you especially like about school?

   _____

   _____

4. What problems do you have at school?

   _____

   _____

5. How did you deal with those problems?

   _____

   _____

6. What have your teachers done in the past that helped you learn and get along with other students?

   _____

   _____

Analysis and Reflection: Make a list of actions teachers could take to ease learning for culturally diverse students. Share your list with fellow students and/or cooperating teachers, and discuss the pros and cons of each suggestion.

Activity 2.5: Teacher Expectations Questionnaire for Students

Purpose: The nature of teacher expectations is an important variable in building positive learning environments. This questionnaire can help you assess your treatment of students.

Directions: Distribute the questionnaire and have students rate each statement on a scale of 1 to 3. Use the smiley face version for younger students.

	1 Seldom	2 Sometimes	3 Always
The Way You See Me Working with You			
1. Do I praise you for good work?	1	2	3
2. Do I like you?	1	2	3
3. Am I friendly?	1	2	3
4. Do I call on you when you raise your hand?	1	2	3
5. Do I criticize you when you don't deserve it?	1	2	3
6. Am I unfriendly?	1	2	3
7. Do I work with you as much as with other students?	1	2	3
8. Do I treat you fairly?	1	2	3
9. Do I smile at you?	1	2	3
10. Do I grade your work fairly?	1	2	3
11. Do I help you when you need help?	1	2	3
12. Do I pay attention to you?	1	2	3
13. Do I understand your problems?	1	2	3
14. Do I like your work?	1	2	3
15. Do I give you enough responsibility?	1	2	3
16. Do you like the way I look at you?	1	2	3
17. Do I give you enough time for your work?	1	2	3
18. Do I ask you "hard" questions?	1	2	3
19. Do you think I am friendly toward you?	1	2	3
20. Do I ask enough from you?	1	2	3

Analysis and Reflection: Find the class mean for each item. Compare the class mean with the mean score for the five most positive students and the five least positive students. Reflect on the differences you see between students who see you most positively and those who see you least positively. Are there racial differences? Gender differences? Social class differences?

Activity 2.6: Portfolio: My Understanding of Policies Related to Student Learning, Diversity, and Inclusion

Purpose: This portfolio exercise will help you gather materials in your portfolio that demonstrate your understanding of student learning, diversity, and inclusion.

Directions: Create a portfolio entry by completing the following steps:

STEP 1:   Select a key component of a school district's or school's current policies related to diversity, inclusion, multicultural education, and student learning. Generally, you can get this information from your principal if you are taking a practicum along with this course. If not, contact the district's central office.

STEP 2:   Observe how these policies are implemented in a classroom, school office, and school cafeteria. You may wish to document your observation with pictures.

STEP 3:   Do a written analysis or picture essay of your findings. Your analysis or essay should include (a) features in each setting that correspond with the policies, (b) features in each setting that show efforts are underway, and (c) features in each setting that still need work.

STEP 4:   Review all your work and place it in your portfolio, along with a hypothetical letter to district personnel describing your insights about diversity, inclusion, and student learning, and how these insights will help you become an effective teacher.

Activity 2.7: Charting the Characteristics of a School's Attendance Boundaries

Purpose: One very important aspect of working with diverse students is to understand the community where they live. The purpose of this activity is to give you practice in gaining familiarity with your community.

Directions: Get an attendance boundary map from a school district for a school's community you want to examine. It may be the school where you have some type of field experience. Spend an afternoon walking and/or driving around the area and make note of the characteristics listed below. (Walking is best.)

1. Make a rough sketch of the area, noting major streets and landmarks.

2. What is the predominant socioeconomic status (SES) of the neighborhood?

    _____

    _____

3. Is this neighborhood's SES (socioeconomic status) homogeneous, or are there pockets of differing SES? What are these? Where are they?

    _____

    _____

4. What conditions are homes in around the neighborhood? Are they mostly apartments, single-family homes, or a mix?

    _____

    _____

5. What ethnic or racial groups are represented in the neighborhood? Which one is the majority group?

    _____

    _____

6. What age groups are represented in the neighborhood? Which is the majority?

    _____

    _____

7. Count the number of places of worship. What religions do they represent? Where are they concentrated?

    _____

    _____

8. What is the economic base of the community? What industries are there? What commercial enterprises? What is the community's level of economic health?

    _____

    _____

9. Does the community contain any centers for the arts or other cultural centers? What is their focus? Where are they located?

    _____

    _____

10. Where are the public libraries located? Stop in the library and skim the local newspaper. Find out if there is a community newspaper. Find out if there is a local history you might read.

    _____

    _____

11. What services does the community provide for children?

    _____

    _____

12. Describe the parks and other recreation facilities.

_____

_____

13. Where are the "hangouts?"

_____

_____

14. How would you characterize the "tone" of the community? Optimistic? Busy? Depressed? Orderly? Unruly? Quiet?

_____

_____

15. What other characteristics of this community stand out for you?

_____

_____

Analysis and Reflection: Write a paragraph about how you might incorporate the knowledge you've obtained about the community into your teaching. How will it help you establish rapport with students? How will it help you develop good working relationships with parents? How can you use the information in your lessons?

CHAPTER 3

TEACHER PLANNING

Activity 3.1   Assessing My Planning Skills
Activity 3.2   Writing Objectives
Activity 3.3   Timetabling Techniques
Activity 3.4   Observing Lesson Activities and Segments
Activity 3.5   Portfolio: Demonstrating My Planning Skills

Activity 3.1: Assessing My Planning Skills

Purpose: This activity will help you assess your level of understanding and skill in various aspects of planning.

Directions: Check the level of understanding or skill you perceive you have for the various concepts and teaching tasks associated with planning for instruction.

Understanding or Skill	Level of Understanding or Skill		
	High	Medium	Low
My understanding of:			
Perspective on planning	____	____	____
Consequences of planning	____	____	____
Planning domains and cycles	____	____	____
Role of instructional objectives	____	____	____
Taxonomies of instructional objectives	____	____	____
My ability to:			
Write instructional objectives	____	____	____
Construct daily lesson plans	____	____	____
Construct unit plans	____	____	____
Construct yearly plans	____	____	____
Make a Gantt chart	____	____	____
Plan for routines	____	____	____
Plan to use time and space	____	____	____

Activity 3.2: Writing Objectives

Purpose: Objectives are an important aspect of teaching practice. Beginners may need to focus their lessons more carefully than experts. For this reason, you must gain facility in writing objectives. This activity will give you practice in writing and evaluating objectives.

Directions: Write eight objectives for your grade level or subject area. Evaluate them using the guide that follows.

1. _____

   _____

2. _____

   _____

3. _____

   _____

4. _____

   _____

5. _____

   _____

6. _____

   _____

7. _____

   _____

8. _____

   _____

Rate each objective good, fair, or poor according to how well it (1) defines the student behavior, (2) prescribes the testing situation, and (3) sets the performance criteria.

	1	2	3	4	5	6	7	8
Objective Number								
Student behavior								
Testing situation								
Performance criteria								

Now rewrite each objective, using the format recommended by Gronlund in Chapter 3, page 114.

Analysis and Reflection: Now revise all objectives as needed. Was there any aspect of objective writing that was especially difficult? What was it? How could you make it easier? Which format did you prefer? Why?

Activity 3.3 Timetabling Techniques

Purpose: Gantt charts can be very helpful time management devices. This activity is to assist you in gaining facility in using Gantt charts.

Directions: Use the guidelines below to plan three different kinds of activities: getting ready for school or work, writing a paper, and arranging a field trip.

Activity	6:00	6:15	6:30	6:45	7:00	7:15	7:30	7:45	8:00	8:15	8:30

1. Think about each activity you must do to get ready for school or work each day. List each activity along the left side of the chart above. Then draw a line horizontally from the beginning to ending time of each activity.
2. Think about all the tasks that need to be done when you are writing a paper for a class. This time, make your own chart. Again, list the activities on the left. Then decide if your time demarcations should be days, weeks, or months and draw a line between the beginning and ending times for each activity.
3. Finally, think about all the things that would need to be done if you were planning a field trip for a class you were teaching. Make your own chart, list the activities, and mark the beginning and ending times for each activity.

Analysis and Reflection: Do you notice any patterns in the way you plan? Are there ways you can facilitate your own planning? For example, are you able to plan efficiently in snatches of time on the subway, waiting in the doctor's office, or waiting for the kettle to boil? Or do you need to set aside a quantity of time and arrange for peace and quiet in order to get your planning done? Write a paragraph on your planning style.

Activity 3.4: Observing Lesson Activities and Segments

Purpose: Activity structures, or lesson segments, form the basic structural units of a lesson. Becoming sensitive to these structures will assist you in your own planning. The purpose of this activity is to help you uncover the internal structure of an experienced teacher's lesson.

Directions: Each time the teacher begins a new lesson segment, record the time the segment begins and the type of activity that occurs during that segment. You may see activities like "lecturing," "checking for understanding," "conducting a discussion," "giving an exam," "demonstrating," and others. Also note the teacher's transition statements and/or actions.

Time	Activity	Transition Statement/Action

Analysis and Reflection: Calculate the amount of time the teacher spent on each segment and each type of activity. Which activities took more time? Which took less? Which transition statements and actions were the most common? Which seemed to work the best?

Activity 3.5: Portfolio: Demonstrating My Planning Skills

Purpose: This activity will provide you with materials for your portfolio that demonstrate your understanding of and skill in planning lessons and units.

Directions: Create a unit plan and a lesson plan by completing the steps that follow:

STEP 1:   Choose a topic from your field that you may want to teach to students in the future.

STEP 2:   Develop a unit plan using the guidelines and format provided on page 123 in Chapter 3.

STEP 3:   Choose a portion of your topic that you believe can be taught in one day. Develop a daily lesson plan for this portion using the guidelines and format provided on page 122.

STEP 4:   Write a brief critique of your unit and lesson plans describing why you chose to approach the topic the way you did and assessing the strengths and weaknesses of your work.

STEP 5:   Arrange your unit, lesson plans, and critique in your portfolio in a way that will let someone understand your grasp of the planning process.

CHAPTER 4

CLASSROOMS AS LEARNING COMMUNITIES

Activity 4.1   Assessing My Ability to Build Productive Learning Communities
Activity 4.2   Surveying Students about Classroom Life
Activity 4.3   Interviewing Teachers about Classroom Goal and Reward Structures
Activity 4.4   Portfolio: My Ideas about Positive Classroom Learning Communities

Activity 4.1: Assessing My Ability to Build Productive Learning Communities

Purpose: This activity will help you assess your level of understanding and skill for building productive learning communities.

Directions: Check the level of understanding or skill you have for the various concepts and teaching tasks listed for building productive learning communities.

Understanding or Skill	Level of Understanding or Skill		
	High	Medium	Low
My understanding of:			
Classroom properties	_____	_____	_____
Classroom processes	_____	_____	_____
Classroom structures	_____	_____	_____
Motivation	_____	_____	_____
My ability to:			
Increase student motivation by . . .			
Attending to alterable factors	_____	_____	_____
Creating positive learning situations	_____	_____	_____
Building on student interests	_____	_____	_____
Accomplishing flow	_____	_____	_____
Using knowledge of results	_____	_____	_____
Attending to student needs and self-determination	_____	_____	_____
Attending to goal and task structures	_____	_____	_____

Understanding or Skill	Level of Understanding or Skill		
	High	Medium	Low
Facilitate group development by attending to . . .			
Inclusion and membership	_____	_____	_____
Rules and routines	_____	_____	_____
Influence and collaboration	_____	_____	_____
Individual and academic achievement	_____	_____	_____
Self-renewal and closure	_____	_____	_____

Activity 4.2: Surveying Students about Classroom Life

Purpose: A positive classroom environment can facilitate learning. This activity will give you a means of determining students' perceptions about classroom life.

Directions: Ask a teacher if you can conduct the survey in his or her class. Then distribute the survey to students for them to fill out in class. If you are working with younger children or those with reading difficulties, you may wish to read each item aloud and have students fill out answer sheets with happy, indifferent, or frowning faces. Add other questions that may be of special interest to you. Tell students their answers will remain confidential.

Classroom Life

Here is a list of some statements that describe life in the classroom. Circle the letter in front of the statement that best tells how you feel about this class. There are no right or wrong answers.

1. Life in this class with your regular teacher has:
    a. All good things
    b. Mostly good things
    c. More good things than bad
    d. About as many good things as bad
    e. More bad things than good
    f. Mostly bad things

2. How hard are you working these days on learning what is being taught at school?
    a. Very hard
    b. Quite hard
    c. Not very hard
    d. Not hard at all

3. When I'm in this class, I usually am:
    a. Wide awake and very interested
    b. Pretty interested, kind of bored part of the time
    c. Not very interested, bored quite a lot of the time
    d. Bored, don't like it

4. How hard are you working on schoolwork compared with the others in the class?
   a. Harder than most
   b. A little harder than most
   c. About the same as most
   d. A little less than most
   e. Quite a bit less than most

5. How many of the pupils in this class do what the teacher suggests?
   a. Most of them do
   b. More than half do
   c. Less than half do
   d. Hardly anybody does

6. If you help each other with your work in this class, the teacher:
   a. Likes it a lot
   b. Likes it some
   c. Likes it a little
   d. Doesn't like it at all

7. How often do the pupils in this class help one another with their schoolwork?
   a. Most of the time
   b. Sometimes
   c. Hardly ever
   d. Never

8. How often do the pupils in this class act friendly toward one another?
   a. Always
   b. Most of the time
   c. Sometimes
   d. Hardly ever

Analysis and Reflection: Tabulate and examine the results of the survey to obtain a broad view of the classroom's tone, student motivation, and norms and expectations of the group. Look for classroom trends and for individuals or subgroups that may deviate from the classroom. Write a paragraph about this classroom's climate and its strong and weak points; suggest ways it might be improved.

Activity 4.3: Interviewing Teachers about Classroom Goal and Reward Structures

Purpose: Goal and reward structures can have a significant impact on the learning environment. This activity is to help you examine how goal and reward structures are exhibited in classrooms.

Directions: Use these questions as a guide in interviewing teachers about how they use classroom goal and reward structures.

(Remember that goal structures can be individualistic, competitive, or cooperative; that is, students' attainment of a goal can be unrelated to others' attainment, dependent on the failure of others, or dependent on the success of others, respectively. Reward structures are distinct from goal structures in that they refer to the rewards students receive for attaining their goals. Reward structures can also be individualistic, competitive, or cooperative. As in goal structures, if rewards are given individually and independently of the rewards others receive, then the reward structure is individualistic; if one's reward is dependent on the failure of others to receive the reward, the reward structure is competitive; and if one's reward is dependent on the success of another, there is a cooperative reward structure. Think about a track meet as an example. If the goal is to win the race, then one person winning means others fail. The ribbon or trophy is the reward. If only the winner receives the ribbon, then the reward structure is competitive. If everyone receives a ribbon, say for participation, then the reward structure is individualistic.)

1. What activities do you have students do in which their ability to complete the activity or attain the goal of the activity is unrelated to whether other students complete it?

   _____

   _____

   _____

   _____

   _____

2. What activities do you have students do in which their ability to complete the activity or attain the goal of the activity depends on other students not completing it or attaining the goal?

   _____

   _____

   _____

3. What activities do you have students do in which they must work together, so that one student's ability to complete the activity and attain the goal depends on other students also being able to complete it and attain the goal?

_____

_____

_____

_____

4. In what ways do you reward students so that one student's reward is unrelated to rewards for any other students?

_____

_____

_____

_____

5. In what ways do you reward students so that one student's reward depends on another student not receiving the award?

_____

_____

_____

_____

6. In what ways do you reward students so that one student's reward hinges on whether other students also receive the reward?

_____

_____

_____

_____

Analysis and Reflection: What are the predominant goal and reward structures in these teachers' classes? Are all three types of structures represented? Is the mix of structures appropriate? What would be a better mix?

Activity 4.4: Portfolio: My Ideas about Positive Classroom Learning Communities

Purpose: This portfolio activity has been designed to help you think about classroom communities and to demonstrate your beliefs about the features of a positive community.

Directions: Create your ideal classroom learning community by completing the steps below:

STEP 1:   Write a two- or three-page paper that describes your ideas about what constitutes an ideal classroom space and environment.

STEP 2:   Illustrate your ideas with artwork or actual pictures. The things you might want to show include:

- How space is used in the classroom.
- How the teacher interacts with students.
- How students interact with one another.

STEP 3:   Write guidelines and steps you think teachers need to follow to create a classroom with a good physical ambiance and a positive learning environment.

STEP 4:   Arrange all of the above in your portfolio in a way that clearly and concisely illustrates your ideas about learning communities.

CHAPTER 5

CLASSROOM MANAGEMENT

Activity 5.1   Assessing My Classroom Management Skills
Activity 5.2   Observing Teachers' Management Behavior
Activity 5.3   Observing Students' Influence on Academic Tasks
Activity 5.4   Interviewing Teachers about Rules and Procedures
Activity 5.5   Observing Management Practices during Unstable Periods
Activity 5.6   Observing Teacher Responses to Student Misbehavior
Activity 5.7   Portfolio: My Classroom Management Platform

Activity 5.1: Assessing My Classroom Management Skills

Purpose: The activities for this chapter begin with an assessment device designed to help you to gauge your level of effectiveness in applying classroom management skills.

Directions: Check the level of effectiveness you feel you have attained for each of the following skills.

Understanding or Skill	Level of Understanding or Skill		
	High	Medium	Low
My understanding of:			
Establish and teach rules and procedures			
Student movement	___	___	___
Student talk	___	___	___
Downtimes	___	___	___
Ensure smoothness and momentum	___	___	___
Orchestrate unstable periods			
Planning thoroughly	___	___	___
Cuing and signaling	___	___	___
Develop student accountability	___	___	___
Manage inappropriate and disruptive behavior			
With-itness	___	___	___
Overlappingness	___	___	___
Using the desist response	___	___	___
Project confidence			
Using rewards	___	___	___
Using punishment	___	___	___
Use the classroom meeting model	___	___	___

Activity 5.2: Observing Teachers' Management Behavior

Purpose: As discussed in Chapter 5, Kounin has contributed much to our under-standing of classroom management. This activity will help you develop awareness of teacher in-class behaviors described by Kounin that have an impact on classroom management.

Directions: Observe a teacher for about an hour. As you observe, note instances in which the lesson seems to go especially well—students are orderly and on task—and instances in which the lesson seems to go especially poorly—students are disorderly and off task. After the observation, answer the following questions.

1. Did the teacher exhibit with-itness? _____

    If so, give an example that appeared during the lesson. _____

    _____

    Describe how students behaved in this example. _____

    _____

    If not, how might he or she have done so? _____

    _____

2. Did the teacher exhibit overlappingness? _____

    If so, give an example that appeared during the lesson. _____

    _____

    Describe how students behaved in this example. _____

    _____

    If not, how might he or she have done so? _____

    _____

3. Did the teacher exhibit smoothness? _____

    If so, give an example that appeared during the lesson. _____

    _____

    Describe how students behaved in this example. _____

    _____

    If not, how might he or she have done so? _____

_____

4. Did the teacher exhibit momentum? _____

    If so, give an example that appeared during the lesson. _____

    _____

    Describe how students behaved in this example. _____

    _____

    If not, how might he or she have done so? _____

    _____

5. Did the teacher exhibit group alerting? _____

    If so, give an example that appeared during the lesson. _____

    _____

    Describe how students behaved in this example. _____

    _____

    If not, how might he or she have done so? _____

    _____

6. Did the teacher exhibit accountability for students? _____

    If so, give an example that appeared during the lesson. _____

    _____

    Describe how students behaved in this example. _____

    _____

    If not, how might he or she have done so? _____

    _____

Analysis and Reflection: Write a paragraph about how you might apply these management principles while teaching in your own subject area or grade level.

Activity 5.3: Observing Students' Influence on Academic Tasks

Purpose: Doyle and Carter showed that students can have an impact on what happens in the classroom. It is clearly important for teachers to be aware of the influence students can exert. This activity will help you to develop awareness of the pattern of academic tasks and student influence in the classroom.

Directions: Observe an elementary classroom for at least half a day, or a secondary classroom for at least three consecutive days. Keep a running account of what happens in the classroom, what the teacher says and does, what the students say and do, and the amount of time spent on each activity. Obtain copies of all handouts. Immediately after each observation, write down any details you noticed but did not have time to include during the observation itself.

Analysis and Reflection: Read through your notes several times. Look for recurring patterns of behavior. Are there any consistencies in the way the teacher introduces a new task? In the way he or she elaborates or explains the task? In the way students react? In the type of task and the length of time it takes to complete? In the way tasks are ended? You may see patterns in other areas. Write an additional two pages about the patterns you observed, and comment on why you think those patterns take the form they do. That is, think about who has influence on academic tasks, based on what you observed, and how that influence is exerted. Does it affect academic tasks in a positive or negative way? Do you think these influences are universal, or are they specific to this particular teacher, group of students, or school? What will you do as a teacher to maintain your awareness of these influences in your own classroom, and what will you do to manage these influences in a positive way?

Activity 5.4: Interviewing Teachers about Rules and Procedures

Purpose: Teaching and enforcing appropriate rules and procedures can prevent or solve the vast majority of management and discipline problems. This activity is to help you gain practical knowledge about what kinds of rules and procedures are needed in classrooms and how these are taught and enforced.

Directions: Interview one elementary teacher, one middle school teacher, or one high school teacher using the questions listed here.

1. What are the rules and procedures in your class that govern student movement?

   _____

   _____

   _____

2. How did you initially develop and teach those rules and procedures?

   _____

   _____

   _____

3. Which ones seem easiest for students to follow? Why? Which ones seem hardest? Why?

   _____

   _____

   _____

4. What do you do to maintain and enforce them?

   _____

   _____

   _____

5. What are the rules and procedures in your class that govern student talking?

_____

_____

_____

6. How did you initially develop and teach those rules and procedures?

_____

_____

_____

7. Which ones seem easiest for students to follow? Why? Which ones seem hardest? Why?

_____

_____

_____

8. What do you do to maintain and enforce them?

_____

_____

_____

9. What are the rules and procedures in your class that govern downtime?

_____

_____

_____

10. How did you initially develop and teach those rules and procedures?

_____

_____

_____

11. Which ones seem easiest for students to follow? Why? Which ones seem hardest? Why?

_____

_____

_____

12. What do you do to maintain and enforce them?

_____

_____

_____

Analysis and Reflection: What seem to be the common elements of rules and procedures at any grade level? Are there any rules and procedures that occur at each level? Are there any common ways they are taught, maintained, and enforced? Are there any common areas of difficulty? Conversely, what did you uncover about rules and procedures that seems to apply only to a particular age group or a particular teacher's style? How will you apply what you have learned to your own teaching?

Activity 5.5: Observing Management Practices during Unstable Periods

Purpose: Unstable periods in classroom life pose the most difficult management challenges. This activity is to help you to gain practical knowledge about how to manage these difficult periods.

Directions: Observe an elementary classroom for a few hours from the opening of the school day, or a secondary classroom for an entire period. Check the actions you see the teacher take in managing unstable periods.

	Yes	No

1. Opening Class

    In order to open class smoothly and efficiently, did the teacher do the following:

    a. Greet students at the door?   ____   ____

       If so, give an example: _____

       _____

    b. Use student helpers for routine administrative tasks?   ____   ____

       If so, give an example: _____

       _____

    c. Write start-up activities on the board?   ____   ____

       If so, give an example:

       _____

    d. Use routine or ceremonial events that set the proper tone?   ____   ____

       If so, give an example:

       _____

    e. Other (specify):

       _____

2. Transitions

    Keep a tally of the number of transitions you observe._____

    Describe one of the transitions you observed. _____

    _____

	Yes	No

In order to move students smoothly and efficiently from one activity to the next, did the teacher do the following:

a. Rely on routinized procedure?   ____   ____

   If so, give an example: _____

   _____

b. Cue or signal the students in some way?   ____   ____

   If so, give an example: _____

   _____

c. Other (specify): _____

   _____

3. Closing Class

   In order to close class smoothly and efficiently, did the teacher do the following:

   a. Leave sufficient time to collect books and papers?   ____   ____

   b. Make assignments early enough to avoid last-minute confusion?   ____   ____

   c. Rely on routine procedures for collecting papers and materials?   ____   ____

   If so, give an example: _____

   _____

   d. Cue students that close of class was approaching?   ____   ____

   e. Other (specify): _____

Analysis and Reflection: Which elements of effective management of unstable periods did this teacher rely on? Which elements were missing? How might this teacher incorporate these missing elements into his or her management routines? Write a paragraph about how you will manage unstable periods in your own classroom.

Activity 5.6: Observing Teacher Responses to Student Misbehavior

Purpose: How to respond to student misbehavior is one of the greatest concerns of beginning teachers. This activity will help you to gain practical knowledge about how to respond to such misbehavior.

Directions: Observe a classroom for 45 to 60 minutes. Whenever you observe an instance of student misbehavior, quickly describe the incident, then use the codes on the next page to code the type of misbehavior and the teacher's response. (You may use more than one code per incident, if necessary.)

Incidents	Student Misbehavior	Teacher Response
1. _____	_____	_____
_____		
2. _____	_____	_____
_____		
3. _____	_____	_____
_____		
4. _____	_____	_____
_____		
5. _____	_____	_____
_____		
6. _____	_____	_____
_____		
7. _____	_____	_____
_____		
8. _____	_____	_____
_____		
9. _____	_____	_____
_____		
10. _____	_____	_____
_____		

Codes for Student Behavior
a. Minor misbehavior
b. Serious misbehavior

Codes for Teacher Responses
a. With-itness: spotted misbehavior early and accurately
b. Overlapping: while teaching
   1. Moved closer to problem student
   2. Made and held eye contact with problem student
   3. Rested hand on student's shoulder
   4. Integrated off-task remark into teaching activities
   5. Other (specify)
c. Used a desist; that is, told the student to stop the misbehavior. The desist was
   1. Clear
   2. Firm
   3. Rough
d. Restated the rule or procedure for the student
e. Had the student identify the rule or procedure
   1. Gave corrective feedback to the student if he or she did not understand the rule
f. Imposed a consequence
g. Changed activity
h. Other

Analysis and Reflection: What were the teacher's most common responses to instances of minor misbehavior? Were these successful? Why or why not? What were the teacher's most common responses to instances of serious misbehavior? Were these successful? Why or why not? Think through the range of options you will be likely to have for responding to misbehavior. Write at least two paragraphs about these options, and the kinds of situations in which they would be appropriately applied.

Activity 5.7: Portfolio: My Classroom Management Platform

Purpose: This portfolio is an extension of the platform you started in Chapter 1. Here, it provides you with the opportunity to describe your current thinking about classroom management.

Directions: Create a platform on the topic of classroom management by doing the following:

STEP 1:   Write a two- or three-page paper that describes your ideas and attitudes for creating a well-managed classroom. This paper should reflect your thinking at this point in time and can be changed later if you wish.

STEP 2:   In your platform, make sure you include:

- What you believe in regard to preventive management.
- What you believe about student discipline.
- Your ideas about the "Caring Classroom."
- Your ideas and attitudes about student self-management.

STEP 3:   Place your paper in your portfolio. You may wish to illustrate your attitudes and ideas with photographs, videos, and other examples as you did in the Chapter 1 portfolio.

CHAPTER 6

ASSESSMENT AND EVALUATION

Activity 6.1   Assessing My Assessment and Evaluation Skills
Activity 6.2   Interviewing Teachers about Their Evaluation and Grading Procedures
Activity 6.3   Constructing a Test Blueprint
Activity 6.4   Analyzing Teacher-Made Tests
Activity 6.5   Reflecting on the Future of Assessment and Evaluation
Activity 6.6   Portfolio: Demonstrating My Skill for Performance Assessment

Activity 6.1: Assessing My Assessment and Evaluation Skills

Purpose: This activity will help you assess your level of understanding and skill in various aspects of assessment and evaluation.

Directions: Check the level of understanding or skill you perceive you have for the various concepts and teaching tasks associated with classroom evaluation and grading.

Understanding or Skill	Level of Understanding or Skill		
	High	Medium	Low
My understanding of:			
Effects of grading	_____	_____	_____
Teacher bias in grading	_____	_____	_____
Importance of grades to parents	_____	_____	_____
Schoolwide use of standardized tests	_____	_____	_____
Norm- and criterion-referenced tests	_____	_____	_____
Principles of testing and grading	_____	_____	_____
My ability to:			
Diagnose students' prior knowledge	_____	_____	_____
Provide corrective feedback to students	_____	_____	_____
Construct essay tests	_____	_____	_____
Construct objective tests	_____	_____	_____
Score tests free from bias	_____	_____	_____
Help reduce test anxiety for students	_____	_____	_____
Develop a "fair" grading system	_____	_____	_____
Use alternative assessment procedures	_____	_____	_____

Activity 6.2: Interviewing Teachers about Their Evaluation and Grading Procedures

Purpose: Using appropriate testing and grading procedures is an important challenge for beginning teachers. This activity will help you to gain practical knowledge about the testing and grading practices currently being used by teachers.

Directions: Interview several teachers using the questions listed here. You may wish to select teachers at different levels: for example, one elementary, one middle school or junior high, and one high school teacher. Or you may wish to select teachers from different subject areas: for example, history, English, physical education, math, and biology.

1. What would you say is the overall philosophy that guides your evaluation and grading program?

   _____

   _____

   _____

2. What aspects of testing and grading do you find most difficult?

   _____

   _____

   _____

3. How much of what you do in testing and grading is influenced by schoolwide or district policies? Can you give me examples? May I see (or have) a copy of the report card used in your school?

   _____

   _____

   _____

4. Since you have been teaching, have you observed any changes in attitudes and procedures associated with testing and grading? How about students—have their attitudes changed?

   _____

   _____

   Have parents' attitudes changed? Have specific procedures used in your school changed?

   _____

   _____

5. Have you used any performance or authentic assessments? If so, how have they worked?

   _____

   _____

   _____

   _____

6. If you had a magic wand and could make anything happen, what would you decree in regard to student evaluation and testing? Why do you choose these actions?

   _____

   _____

   _____

   _____

Activity 6.3: Constructing a Test Blueprint

Purpose: A question that confronts all teachers is what to cover on a test. Students want to know what will be on a test so they know what to study. Teachers want to make sure they test various levels of student understanding; they also want to make their tests congruent with their instructional objectives. The "test blueprint" is one device developed by evaluation specialists to assist with test construction. This activity has been designed to give you practice with making a test blueprint.

Directions: Select a unit from a curriculum guide in your subject area or two or three chapters from a textbook that you might use. If you have previously developed a unit of work on your own, you may wish to use it.

Using the table below construct a test blueprint. You may want to look at the example provided on page 234 in *Learning to Teach*. List your objectives at the bottom of the table and then identify the type and number of test items or other assessment devices in each of the cells. Note that the rows in the table represent the various knowledge dimensions of Bloom's Revised Taxonomy and the columns are the cognitive processes found in the taxonomy.

			Cognitive Processes			
Knowledge Dimension	**Remember**	**Understand**	**Apply**	**Analyze**	**Evaluate**	**Create**
Factual Knowledge						
Conceptual Knowledge						
Procedural Knowledge						
Metacognitive Knowledge						

Activity 6.4: Analyzing Teacher-Made Tests

Purpose: Making good tests is hard work. Some teachers do this task better than others. This tool is to help you gain practical knowledge about tests constructed by teachers.

Directions: Obtain a copy of a test constructed by a teacher, either one of the teachers you have interviewed previously, a teacher with whom you are doing a practicum, or one of your college professors.

Using the chart like the one below, perform three tasks. List in the left-hand column each question on the test and classify it as to its type (essay, multiple-choice, matching, etc.). Then make a tick in the cell of the chart that most accurately classifies the test item according to its knowledge dimension and cognitive process. You will note that the rows in the chart represent the various knowledge dimensions of Bloom's Revised Taxonomy and the columns are the cognitive processes found in the taxonomy.

		Cognitive Processes					
Test Item	Knowledge Dimension	Remember	Understand	Apply	Analyze	Evaluate	Create
	Factual Knowledge						
	Conceptual Knowledge						
	Procedural Knowledge						
	Metacognitive Knowledge						

Analysis and Reflection: Are most items in one cell, such as remembering factual information, or are they spread across a number of cells? How do you explain the pattern you found? How might these patterns influence you as you construct your own tests?

Activity 6.5: Reflecting on the Future of Assessment and Evaluation

Purpose: This activity will help you think about the future of evaluation and grading.

Directions: Reflect on the items listed here and suggest changes you would make in current assessment, evaluation, and grading practices.

1. List all current evaluation and grading practices you think are beneficial to students and their learning.

   _____

   _____

2. Now list all practices you think are, although not harmful, nonetheless *not* beneficial to students and their learning.

   _____

   _____

3. Finally, list all practices you think are harmful or destructive to students and their learning.

   _____

   _____

4. Reflect on the three lists you have just made. What do they tell you about your own personal dispositions toward evaluation and grading?

   _____

   _____

5. Give yourself a magic wand; in the space below, describe the evaluation program you would decree if it were completely up to you.

   _____

   _____

6. Think for a moment about the program you have devised. What do you think might be the major impediments to its implementation? How could these impediments be overcome?

   _____

   _____

Activity 6.6: Portfolio: Demonstrating My Skill for Performance Assessment

Purpose: This portfolio activity will provide you with materials for your portfolio that demonstrate your understanding of and skill in developing and using some form of performance assessment.

Directions: Create a performance assessment device and compare it to a more traditional test by completing the steps that follow.

STEP 1:   Choose some topic or question from your field for which students can demonstrate their understanding or skill through some type of performance test.

STEP 2:   Develop a traditional paper-and-pencil test to measure the understanding or skill. (Use test guidelines on pp. 235–238).

STEP 3:   Next, develop a performance assessment and a scoring rubric for the same topic. Go back to Figures 6.6 and 6.7 for examples of how to do this.

STEP 4:   Give both assessment devices to a few students you know. These could be students in a school where you have a practicum or they could be your college classmates.

STEP 5:   Write a brief critique of your performance assessment describing its strengths and weaknesses. Also, provide your ideas about the use of performance assessment in your teaching field.

STEP 6:   Arrange your assessment devices and your critique in your portfolio in a way that will let someone understand your grasp of performance assessment in a brief amount of time.

CHAPTER 7

PRESENTATION

Activity 7.1   Assessing My Presentation Skills
Activity 7.2   Lesson Plan for Presentation
Activity 7.3   Observing a Presentation in Microteaching or Classrooms
Activity 7.4   Observing Teacher Clarity
Activity 7.5   Portfolio: Creating My Own Presentation Lesson Using an
                Advance Organizer

Activity 7.1: Assessing My Presentation Skills

Purpose: This activity provides an overall indication of your skill in the presentation model. The key components of the model, as given in the text, are highlighted here. This could be used just after reading the chapter to pinpoint areas of confusion or after a practice presentation to assess your own performance.

Directions: Check the level of skill you perceive that you have for the various teaching tasks associated with the presentation model.

Understanding or Skill	Level of Understanding or Skill		
	High	Medium	Low
Preinstructional tasks:			
Choosing content	_____	_____	_____
Determining students' prior knowledge	_____	_____	_____
Selecting an advance organizer	_____	_____	_____
Instructional tasks:			
Phase 1: Explaining goals and establishing set	_____	_____	_____
Phase 2: Presenting the advance organizer	_____	_____	_____
Phase 3: Presenting the learning materials			
Clarity	_____	_____	_____
Explaining links and examples	_____	_____	_____
Enthusiasm	_____	_____	_____
Phase 4: Checking for and strengthening thinking			
Questioning	_____	_____	_____
Discussing	_____	_____	_____
Postinstructional tasks			
Testing and grading	_____	_____	_____
Assessing my own performance	_____	_____	_____

Activity 7.2: Lesson Plan for Presentation

Purpose: This is a suggested format for making a lesson plan tailored specifically to the presentation model. You can try it out as you plan a presentation microteaching assignment or in field placements. As you do so, maintain an attitude of flexibility and experimentation. Revise the format as you see the need.*

Directions: Follow the guidelines below as you plan a presentation lesson.

Planning phase

Content to be taught: _____

_____

Advance organizer: _____

_____

Objectives

1. Given _____, the student will be able to
            (*situation*)

_____
                        (*target behavior*)

with _____

_____.
                        (*level of performance*)

2. Given _____ the student will be able to
            (*situation*)

_____
                        (*target behavior*)

with_____

_____.
                        (*level of performance*)

_____

*A more elaborate planning activity for presentation lessons is available on the *Interactive Student CD-ROM*.

Conducting the lesson

Time	Phase and Activities	Materials
_____	Lesson goals, rationale, and set: _____	

_____

_____

_____ Advance organizer: _____

_____

_____

_____ Presenting information: _____

_____

_____

_____ Checking for understanding and strengthening student thinking:

_____

_____

Pitfalls to avoid

During Introduction	During Transitions	During Ending

Analysis and Reflection: How well did this format work for you? Did some elements seem to be extraneous to you? Did some important elements seem to be missing? How will you revise this format the next time you give a presentation? Write a paragraph in response to these questions.

Activity 7.3: Observing a Presentation in Microteaching or Classrooms

Directions: This form highlights the key aspects of a presentation lesson. It can be used to observe a peer in a microteaching laboratory or an experienced classroom teacher. It can also be used to assess a lesson you have taught and videotaped. As you observe the lesson, check the category you believe describes the level of performance of the teacher you are observing. Also answer the general questions about the lesson at the bottom of the form.

Teacher Behavior	Level of Performance			
	Excellent	Acceptable	Needs Improvement	Not Needed
Planning:				
How appropriate was the content of the lesson?	_____	_____	_____	_____
How well prepared was the teacher overall?	_____	_____	_____	_____
Execution:				
How well did the teacher explain goals and purposes?	_____	_____	_____	_____
Establish set?	_____	_____	_____	_____
Provide the advance organizer?	_____	_____	_____	_____
Speak with clarity?	_____	_____	_____	_____
Use explaining links and examples?	_____	_____	_____	_____
Display appropriate enthusiasm?	_____	_____	_____	_____
Check for understanding and strengthen student thinking?	_____	_____	_____	_____

Overall planning

What did you like best about the way the lesson was planned and organized?

_____

_____

What could be improved?

_____

_____

Lesson execution

Think about teaching style and delivery. What did you like best about the way the lesson was presented?

_____

_____

What could be improved?

_____

_____

If you were a student in peer microteaching, how did you feel about the teacher's interaction with you?

_____

_____

SOURCE: After a plan used by faculty at Augsburg College.

Activity 7.4: Observing Teacher Clarity

Purpose: This activity refines understanding of how to achieve clarity. As described in the chapter, clarity has several ingredients, such as checking for student understanding and avoiding vagueness. These ingredients are listed here.

Directions: Observe a teacher during a presentation for 10 to 15 minutes, then check how effectively you feel the teacher incorporated these indicators of clarity into his or her presentation.

Indicators of Clarity	Level of Effectiveness			
	High	Medium	Low	Not Done
Stated objectives	____	____	____	____
Made content organization explicit	____	____	____	____
Used explaining links	____	____	____	____
Gave appropriate examples	____	____	____	____
Used the rule-example-rule technique	____	____	____	____
Used a variety of media	____	____	____	____
Made smooth transitions from one point to the next	____	____	____	____
Checked with students to verify understanding	____	____	____	____
Avoided vagueness	____	____	____	____
Other (specify) _____	____	____	____	____

Analysis and Reflection: Write specific examples from the teacher's presentation that reflect each indicator of clarity. Can you apply any of these examples to your own subject area or grade level? How might you adapt the others to fit your subject or grade level? Keep these ideas on file for future use.

Activity 7.5: Portfolio: Creating My Own Presentation Lesson Using an Advance Organizer

Purpose: It is always difficult to teach a new idea to someone. The purposes of this portfolio assignment are to help you gain skill in designing a lesson for teaching a new idea to someone and to develop a product that can become a part of your portfolio.

Directions: Follow the steps here to design and teach a lesson and to display it in your portfolio.

STEP 1:   Choose an individual (friend, family member, student at your practicum site) who would allow you to teach them something.

STEP 2:   Choose a chunk of factual and conceptual knowledge that you think this person doesn't know very much about. It may be knowledge from your teaching field, or it could be associated with some hobby or interest you have.

STEP 3:   Develop goals and design a lesson to teach the knowledge to the individual you identified in step 1 using the presentation model. In your lesson plan, outline what you will do at each phase of the model's syntax. Pay particular attention to how you are going to design and use an advance organizer.

STEP 4:   Teach the lesson to the individual and capture what you do with a camcorder or a 35mm camera and/or an audiotape.

STEP 5:   View or listen to the video- or audiotape and write a critique of your lesson. How appropriate was the knowledge you selected for the individual you taught? How did the individual react to your advance organizer? What do you think of your advance organizer? Did the lesson turn out as you planned it? What would you do differently next time? What did this experience teach you about presentation teaching and the use of advance organizers?

STEP 6:   Arrange the following in your portfolio: your lesson plan, your advance organizer, pictures of you conducting the lesson, and your critique.

CHAPTER 8

DIRECT INSTRUCTION

Activity 8.1   Assessing My Skills for Using the Direct Instruction Model
Activity 8.2   Lesson Plan Format for a Direct Instruction Model Lesson
Activity 8.3   Observing Direct Instruction in Microteaching or Classrooms
Activity 8.4   Observing Teacher Use of Practice
Activity 8.5   Portfolio: Showing My Use of Task Analysis and Demonstration

Activity 8.1: Assessing My Skills for Using the Direct Instruction Model

Purpose: To help you gain insight into your level of skill in using the model, do this activity after reading the chapter or after a microteaching or field assignment.

Directions: Check the level of skill you perceive yourself having for the various teaching tasks associated with the direct instruction model.

Understanding or Skill	Level of Understanding or Skill		
	High	Medium	Low
Planning tasks:			
Writing clear objectives	_____	_____	_____
Performing task analysis	_____	_____	_____
Preparing skill lessons	_____	_____	_____
Preparing for demonstration	_____	_____	_____
Instructional tasks:			
Phase 1			
Explaining goals and establishing set	_____	_____	_____
Phase 2			
Conducting demonstration	_____	_____	_____
Phase 3			
Designing guided practice	_____	_____	_____
Phase 4			
Checking for understanding	_____	_____	_____
Providing feedback	_____	_____	_____
Postinstructional tasks:			
Phase 5			
Designing independent practice	_____	_____	_____
Designing performance test items	_____	_____	_____

Activity 8.2: Lesson Plan Format for a Direct Instruction Model Lesson

Purpose: This is a lesson plan format suggested for use with the model. As with the formats suggested for other teaching models, experiment with this format to determine if it meets your requirements. Be flexible and modify it as the need arises.*

Directions: Use the following suggested format as a model for writing a training lesson.

Planning phase
   Content or skill to be taught: _____

_____.

Objectives

   1. Given _____, the student will be able to
                    (*situation*)

   _____.
                              (*target behavior*)

   with _____

   _____.
                              (*level of performance*)

   2. Given _____ the student will be able to
                    (*situation*)

   _____.
                              (*target behavior*)

   with _____

   _____.
                              (*level of performance*)

---

*A more elaborate planning activity for direct instruction is available on the *Interactive Student CD-ROM*.

Conducting the lesson

Time	Phase and Activities	Materials
_____	Lesson objectives and set: _____	
	_____	
_____	Lesson demonstration: _____	
	_____	
_____	Initial guided practice: _____	
	_____	
_____	Checking for understanding and providing feedback: _____	
	_____	
_____	Independent practice activities: _____	
	_____	

Pitfalls to avoid

During Introduction	During Transitions	During Ending

_____

Analysis and Reflection: How well did this format work for you? Did some elements seem to be extraneous to you? Did some important elements seem to be missing? How will you revise this format the next time you give a direct instruction lesson? Write a paragraph in response to these questions.

Activity 8.3: Observing Direct Instruction in Microteaching or Classrooms

Purpose: This form highlights the key aspects of the direct instruction model. It can be used to observe a peer in a microteaching laboratory or an experienced classroom teacher. It can also be used to assess a lesson you have taught and videotaped.

Directions: As you observe the lesson, check the category you believe describes the level of performance of the teacher you are observing. Also answer the general questions about the lesson at the bottom of the form.

Teacher Behavior	Level of Performance			
	Excellent	Acceptable	Needs Improvement	Not Needed
Planning:				
How appropriate was the skill selected to teach?	_____	_____	_____	_____
How well prepared was the teacher overall?	_____	_____	_____	_____
How well had the teacher performed task analysis?	_____	_____	_____	_____
Execution:				
How well did the teacher				
Explain goals and purposes?	_____	_____	_____	_____
Establish set?	_____	_____	_____	_____
Demonstrate the skill or material?	_____	_____	_____	_____
Provide for initial practice?	_____	_____	_____	_____
Check for student understanding?	_____	_____	_____	_____
Provide feedback to students?	_____	_____	_____	_____
Try to promote transfer?	_____	_____	_____	_____
Provide for independent practice?	_____	_____	_____	_____

Overall planning

What did you like best about the way the lesson was planned and organized?

_____

What could be improved?

_____

Lesson execution

Think about teaching style and delivery. What did you like best about the way the lesson was presented?

_____

What could be improved?

_____

Activity 8.4: Observing Teacher Use of Practice

Purpose: Practice is an important element in the direct instruction model and requires finesse to manage properly. Do this activity in the field to help refine your understanding of the use of practice.

Directions: During skill lessons, observe a teacher each day for several days. Stay in the same subject area, and try to observe from the first day a skill is introduced to the last day it is covered. For example, you may watch a teacher introduce, develop, and review the skill of writing a business letter, multiplying by 5s, or cleaning a carburetor. Whatever the skill, pay close attention to how the teacher handles student practice. Use the questions below to guide your observation and reflection.

1. On the first day the skill was introduced, what type of practice assignment did the teacher make: guided practice, independent practice, or both?

   _____

   How much time was devoted to the practice segment in class?

   _____

   As homework? _____

   What proportion of the total lesson was devoted to practice? _____

   Describe the teacher's behavior during the practice segment.

   _____

   _____

   Describe the students' behavior during the practice segment.

   _____

   _____

2. As the skill was developed over one or a few days, what type of practice assignment did the teacher make: guided practice, independent practice, or both?

   _____

   _____

   How much time was devoted to the practice segment in class?

   _____

   As homework? _____

   What proportion of the total lesson was devoted to practice? _____

Describe the teacher's behavior during the practice segment.

_____

_____

Describe the students' behavior during the practice segment.

_____

_____

3. As the skill was reviewed, what type of practice assignment did the teacher make: guided practice, independent practice, or both?

_____

_____

How much time was devoted to the practice segment in class?

_____

As homework? _____

What proportion of the total lesson was devoted to practice? _____

Describe the teacher's behavior during the practice segment.

_____

_____

Describe the students' behavior during the practice segment.

_____

_____

Analysis and Reflection: How did the teacher portion out practice? In other words, did you see massed or distributed practice, or both? At what points in the development of the skill were these observed: early on, during the development phase, or during review? Did the teacher give an indication that practice assignments were being matched to students' developing ability to perform the skill? If so, how did the teacher gauge student performance? What kinds of teacher behavior characterized earlier skill lessons? Later skill lessons? What kinds of student behavior characterized earlier skill lessons? Later skill lessons? Do you think this teacher made wise decisions concerning provision for student practice? Why or why not?

Activity 8.5: Portfolio: Showing My Use of Task Analysis and Demonstration

Purpose: This exercise will help you gain skill in performing task analysis and conducting demonstrations and develop products of this work for your portfolio.

Directions: Following the steps here, perform a task analysis, conduct a demonstration of some specific skill, and find a means to visually document your work in the portfolio.

STEP 1:   Choose a topic from your teaching field that consists of a number of skills. Do a task analysis identifying all the sub-skills associated with the topic. For example, if you choose ice hockey, some of the sub-skills associated with that sport are dressing with proper equipment, ability to stand on ice, gliding forward, gliding backward, and passing while moving.

STEP 2:   Put the sub-skills in some logical order showing how they relate to one another or how some are prerequisite to others. Do this with some type of flowchart or diagram. This diagram should be done carefully so it can be included in your portfolio.

STEP 3:   Select one skill and prepare a 5- to 10-minute lesson to demonstrate it to a particular audience. The audience may be a group of students, peers in your college classroom, or family members. Your lesson should also be placed in your portfolio.

STEP 4:   Conduct the demonstration after making arrangements to record it visually. This can be done with a camcorder or a 35mm camera. This visual record of the lesson should be placed in your portfolio.

STEP 5:   Critique your task analysis and demonstration. How appropriate was the skill you selected to demonstrate? Did the demonstration work as you planned? What would you do differently next time?

STEP 6:   Arrange the following in your portfolio: the task analysis, the demonstration lesson, pictures of you conducting the demonstration, and your critique.

CHAPTER 9

CONCEPT TEACHING

Activity 9.1   Assessing My Skills for Concept Teaching
Activity 9.2   Observing a Concept Attainment Lesson in Microteaching or Classrooms
Activity 9.3   Concept Analysis
Activity 9.4   Analyzing Curriculum Guides for Concept Lessons
Activity 9.5   Portfolio: Demonstrating My Webbing Skills

Activity 9.1: Assessing My Skills for Concept Teaching

Purpose: The purpose of this activity is to give you an opportunity to assess your current level of effectiveness or understanding of concept teaching.

Directions: Check the level of effectiveness or understanding you feel you have for the teaching tasks listed below that are associated with concept teaching.

Understanding or Skill	Level of Understanding or Skill		
	High	Medium	Low
Planning tasks:			
Select concepts	_____	_____	_____
Define concepts	_____	_____	_____
Analyze concepts	_____	_____	_____
Sequence examples and non-examples	_____	_____	_____
Decide on which approach to use	_____	_____	_____
Instructional tasks:			
Directed presentation			
Present goals and establish set	_____	_____	_____
Name concept and provide definition	_____	_____	_____
Identify critical attributes	_____	_____	_____
Show examples	_____	_____	_____
Develop concept	_____	_____	_____
Analyze thought processes and/or integrate learning	_____	_____	_____

Understanding or Skill	Level of Understanding or Skill		
	High	Medium	Low
Concept attainment			
Present goals and establish set	_____	_____	_____
Present examples and non-examples of concept	_____	_____	_____
Facilitate students' hypothesizing about concept and comparing attributes	_____	_____	_____
Facilitate students' describing how they arrived at the label for the concept	_____	_____	_____
Check for student understanding	_____	_____	_____
Analyze thought processes and/or integrate learning	_____	_____	_____
Postinstructional tasks:			
Test for concept learning	_____	_____	_____

Note: A more elaborate planning activity for concept teaching is available on the *Interactive Student CD-ROM.*

Activity 9.2: Observing a Concept Attainment Lesson in Microteaching or Classrooms

Purpose: This form highlights the key aspects of a concept attainment lesson. It can be used to observe a peer in a microteaching laboratory or an experienced classroom teacher. It can also be used to assess a lesson you have taught and videotaped.

Directions: As you observe the lesson, check the category you believe describes the level of performance of the teacher you are observing. Also answer the general questions about the lesson at the bottom of the form.

Teacher Behavior	Level of Performance			
	Excellent	Acceptable	Needs Improvement	Not Needed
Planning:				
How appropriate was the concept of the lesson?	_____	_____	_____	_____
How well prepared was the teacher overall?	_____	_____	_____	_____
Execution:				
How well did the teacher:				
Explain goals and purposes?	_____	_____	_____	_____
Establish set?	_____	_____	_____	_____
Explain the functions of yes and no categories?	_____	_____	_____	_____
Have sufficient yes and no examples?	_____	_____	_____	_____
Ask questions to focus student thinking on the essential attributes?	_____	_____	_____	_____
Ask students to compare characteristic yes examples?	_____	_____	_____	_____
Ask students to generate hypotheses about the concept?	_____	_____	_____	_____
Have the students name the concept?	_____	_____	_____	_____
Have students provide their own examples and non-examples after concept was defined?	_____	_____	_____	_____
Have students describe the thinking processes they used in attaining the concept?	_____	_____	_____	_____
Have students evaluate the effectiveness of their thinking strategies?	_____	_____	_____	_____

Overall planning

What did you like best about the way the lesson was planned and organized?

_____

_____

What could be improved?

_____

_____

Lesson execution

Think about teaching style and delivery. What did you like best about the way the lesson was presented?

_____

_____

What could be improved?

_____

_____

Activity 9.3: Concept Analysis

Purpose: It is imperative that a teacher carefully analyze any concept he or she is planning to teach. In order to communicate clearly to students what the concept is, what its attributes are, and what constitutes an example or non-example, the teacher needs to have an unshakably clear grasp of the concept. Use this activity as a planning guide to assist you in concept analysis.

Directions: Select a concept for analysis that it is likely you will want to teach some day. Follow the steps listed below to analyze this concept.

1. Name the concept.

   _____

   _____

2. Define or state the rule for the concept.

   _____

   _____

3. List the critical attributes of the concept.

   _____

   _____

4. List the noncritical attributes that are related to the concept.

   _____

   _____

5. Select examples that highlight the critical attributes of the concept.

   _____

   _____

6. Select non-examples that are closely related to the concept.

   _____

   _____

Analysis and Reflection: Try teaching your concept informally to a few friends. Did you discover any parts that were difficult for them to understand? Based on your friends' feedback, refine your definition, attributes, and examples. Write a paragraph on what you learned about forming clear definitions, attributes, and examples.

Activity 9.4: Analyzing Curriculum Guides for Concept Lessons

Purpose: There are always more concepts that could be taught than there is time to teach. The purpose of this activity is to give you practice in making concept selection decisions.

Directions: Obtain a teacher's guide to a textbook in your subject area or grade level. Assume that you are planning a three-week unit on a major topic presented in the text. Select five concepts associated with this topic for inclusion in the unit based on the following:

STEP 1:   List the main objectives for the unit and the key vocabulary (concepts).

STEP 2:   List the concepts that are common to the vocabulary and main objectives list. These are probably the concepts that need to be developed by the teacher.

STEP 3:   From the content of each lesson, select the five concepts to be taught and the sequencing of these concept lessons. Some may be developed prior to the lesson or, as in the case of the graphics organizer, taught concurrent with the lesson.

STEP 4:   Chart the five concepts using the format recommended in *Learning to Teach*.

STEP 5:   Decide which model of concept teaching you will use to teach each concept.

Analysis and Reflection: What factors did you consider in making these decisions? Was the time available an important consideration? Students' prior knowledge? Availability of resources? Other considerations? Did you overlook any factors you should have weighed? Write a paragraph about the factors that enter into concept decisions.

Activity 9.5: Portfolio: Demonstrating My Webbing Skills

Purpose: This exercise will help you gain skill in making conceptual webs and develop products of this work for your portfolio.

Directions: Following the steps here, construct a conceptual web for your portfolio. You may want to refer back to the chapter for more information about how to construct conceptual webs.

STEP 1:   Select a concept for analysis that you might want to teach some day.

STEP 2:   Place the concept in a circle (the core) on a piece of paper.

STEP 3:   Draw strands branching out from the core. These are critical attributes. Give each attribute a name.

STEP 4:   Draw lines connecting the various strands to show how the attributes and dimensions are differentiated from one another.

STEP 5:   Tie the various strands together to show relationships among the attributes.

STEP 6:   Critique your web in a way that will show a potential employer that you understand webbing and its role in planning for a concept lesson.

STEP 7:   Arrange your conceptual web and critique in your portfolio. You may want to add illustrations and pictures to make your work more attractive and eye-catching.

CHAPTER 10

COOPERATIVE LEARNING

Activity 10.1   Assessing My Skills for Using Cooperative Learning
Activity 10.2   Observing Cooperative Learning in Microteaching or Classrooms
Activity 10.3   Observing Small-Group Interaction
Activity 10.4   Observing Transitions and Group Management
Activity 10.5   Visiting the School's Library, Media Center, and/or Computer Laboratory
Activity 10.6   Portfolio: Creating Your Own Lesson for Teaching Social Skills

Activity 10.1: Assessing My Skills for Using Cooperative Learning

Purpose: To help you assess your level of skill in using cooperative learning, this activity can be used either after reading the chapter or after a microteaching or field assignment.

Directions: Check the level of skill you perceive that you have for the various teaching tasks associated with the cooperative learning model.

Understanding or Skill	Level of Understanding or Skill		
	High	Medium	Low
Preinstructional tasks:			
Choosing appropriate content and approach	_____	_____	_____
Deciding on composition of learning teams	_____	_____	_____
Developing and/or gathering needed materials	_____	_____	_____
Writing clear directions	_____	_____	_____
Instructional tasks:			
Explaining objectives and establishing set	_____	_____	_____
Presenting information (lecture and/or text)	_____	_____	_____
Making transition to learning teams	_____	_____	_____
Helping students during team study	_____	_____	_____
Postinstructional tasks:			
Constructing appropriate tests	_____	_____	_____
Scoring tests for individuals and groups	_____	_____	_____
Devising means to recognize student achievement	_____	_____	_____

Activity 10.2: Observing Cooperative Learning in Microteaching or Classrooms

Purpose: This form highlights the key aspects of a cooperative learning lesson. It can be used to observe a peer in a microteaching laboratory or an experienced classroom teacher. It can also be used to assess a lesson you have taught and videotaped.

Directions: As you observe the lesson, check the category you believe describes the level of performance of the teacher you are observing. Also answer the general questions about the lesson at the bottom of the form.

	Level of Performance			
Teacher Behavior	Excellent	Acceptable	Needs Improvement	Not Needed
Planning:				
How appropriate was the content for the lesson?	_____	_____	_____	_____
How appropriate were plans for team formation?	_____	_____	_____	_____
How appropriate were materials gathered to support the lesson?	_____	_____	_____	_____
How well prepared was the teacher overall?	_____	_____	_____	_____
Execution:				
How well did the teacher:				
Explain goals and purposes?	_____	_____	_____	_____
Establish set?	_____	_____	_____	_____
Explain small-group activities?	_____	_____	_____	_____
Make transition to learning teams?	_____	_____	_____	_____
Help students during team study?	_____	_____	_____	_____
Recognize individual effort?	_____	_____	_____	_____
Recognize team effort?	_____	_____	_____	_____

Overall planning

What did you like best about the way the lesson was planned and organized?

_____

_____

What could be improved?

_____

_____

Lesson execution

Think about teaching style and delivery. What did you like best about the way the lesson was presented?

_____

_____

What could be improved?

_____

_____

Activity 10.3: Observing Small-Group Interaction

Purpose: For cooperative learning to be a success, students must help each other learn. This tool will focus on how students behave when in their teams and will enhance your ability to spot off-task behavior.

Directions: Observe a class during the team study phase of a cooperative learning lesson. Watch one of the teams; every 15 seconds, check off which of the following behaviors it exhibits.

Frequency	Group Activity
_____	1. Reading (finding information and so forth)
_____	2. Manipulating equipment
_____	3. Task discussion, general participation
_____	4. Task discussion, one or two students dominate
_____	5. Procedural discussion
_____	6. Observing
_____	7. Nontask discussion
_____	8. Procedural dispute
_____	9. Substantive discussion, task relevant
_____	10. Silence or confusion
_____	11. Off task behaviors
_____	12. Other (specify)

Analysis and Reflection: Were the students more often on or off task? If on task, what did the teacher do that contributed to on-task behavior? If off task, what could the teacher have done to prevent the off-task behavior?

Activity 10.4: Observing Transitions and Group Management

Purpose: As noted in this chapter, managing the transition from large- to small-group work can be trying. This activity will help you focus on teacher behaviors that smooth transition periods.

Directions: Make a check when you observe the teacher performing the indicated behaviors.

_____ Teacher wrote key steps of the activity on the chalkboard or on charts.

_____ Teacher stated directions clearly.

_____ Teacher summarized directions.

_____ Teacher had one or two students summarize directions.

_____ Teacher used hand signals, other signals, or auditory signals to cue students.

_____ Teacher directed teams to the areas of the room where they were to work.

_____ Teacher labeled teamwork areas clearly.

_____ Other (specify) _____

_____

Analysis and Reflection: What key thing did the teacher do to help with transitions? What could the teacher have done to make transition go more smoothly? Why?

Activity 10.5: Visiting the School's Library, Media Center, and/or Computer Laboratory

Purpose: A vital component of the group investigation approach to cooperative learning is an adequate supply of resources that students can comb for information. This activity is designed to assist you in evaluating a school's library or other source facility.

Directions: Visit a school library or other source facility, such as a media center or computer laboratory, and interview resource specialists. Find answers to the following questions.

1. Does the library have a substantial or minimal collection of print materials for student use?

   _____

2. To what degree does the media center or computer laboratory have materials and equipment available for student use?

   _____

3. If you were an elementary or secondary school student, would you find the library, media center, or computer laboratory a pleasant and conducive place to study? Why? Why not?

   _____

   _____

4. What types of procedures does the librarian or specialist prefer when working with a teacher on group projects?

   a. Policy about deadlines?

   _____

   _____

   b. Policy about taking materials to the classroom?

   _____

   _____

   c. Policy about small groups of students coming to the library on their own?

   _____

   d. Policy about computer use? Use of Internet?

   _____

   _____

   e. Policy about resource specialists coming into the room and assisting students with their group investigations?

   _____

   _____

5. What are the main logistical drawbacks or weaknesses of the library, media center, or computer laboratory as a support system for group investigation?

   _____

   _____

Activity 10.6: Portfolio: Creating Your Own Lesson for Teaching Social Skills

Purpose: Teaching social skills is an important and sometimes difficult aspect of a teacher's work. The purpose of this activity is to help you gain skill in designing a social skills lesson and to develop products of this work that can become part of your teaching portfolio.

Directions: Follow the steps below to design a social skills lesson, teach that lesson, and display it in words and pictures in your portfolio.

STEP 1:   Choose a social skill such as cooperation, listening to others, or helping others with their work, and design a short lesson to introduce students to that skill. Do a task analysis of the skill (as described in Chapter 8), identifying all the sub-skills associated with the overall skill.

STEP 2:   Put the sub-skills in some logical order, showing how they relate to one another and those that might be prerequisite to others. Do this with some type of flowchart or web.

STEP 3:   Select one of the sub-skills, and prepare a short lesson to demonstrate the skill to a particular audience. It may be a group of students, peers in your college classroom, or family members. The lesson plan you create should also be placed in your portfolio.

STEP 4:   Teach the social skill, and capture what you do with a camcorder or a 35 mm camera. Place this visual record of the lesson in your portfolio.

STEP 5:   Critique your social skill lesson. How appropriate was the selected social skill for your audience? Did the lesson turn out as you planned it? What would you do differently next time?

STEP 6:   Arrange the following in your portfolio: the task analysis of the social skill, your lesson plan, pictures of you conducting the lesson, and your critique.

CHAPTER 11

PROBLEM-BASED LEARNING

Activity 11.1   Assessing My Skills for Problem-Based Instruction
Activity 11.2   Lesson Plan Format for Problem-Based Learning Instruction
Activity 11.3   Observing Problem-Based Learning in Microteaching or Classrooms
Activity 11.4   Interviewing Teachers about Their Use of Problem-Based Learning
Activity 11.5   Portfolio: Designing and Illustrating Problem Situations

Activity 11.1: Assessing My Skills for Problem-Based Learning

Purpose: This activity provides an overall indication of your skill in understanding and using the problem-based model. The key components of the model, as given in the text, are highlighted here. This could be used just after reading the chapter to pinpoint areas of confusion, or after a practice presentation to assess your own performance.

Directions: Check the level of skill you perceive that you have for the various teaching tasks associated with the problem-based learning model.

Understanding or Skill	Level of Understanding or Skill		
	High	Medium	Low
Preinstructional tasks:			
Choosing content for PBL lesson	_____	_____	_____
Deciding on PBL objectives	_____	_____	_____
Designing problem situations	_____	_____	_____
Organizing resources and logistics	_____	_____	_____
Instructional tasks:			
Phase 1: Orienting students to the problem	_____	_____	_____
Phase 2: Organizing students for study	_____	_____	_____
Phase 3: Assisting student investigations	_____	_____	_____
Phase 4: Helping students develop artifacts/exhibits	_____	_____	_____
Phase 5: Evaluating PBL processes	_____	_____	_____
Postinstructional tasks:			
Assessing student growth	_____	_____	_____
Assessing group efforts	_____	_____	_____
Assessing my own performance	_____	_____	_____

Activity 11.2: Lesson Plan Format for Project-Based Instruction Lesson

Purpose: This is a suggested format for making a lesson plan tailored specifically to planning requirements of the problem-based teaching model. You can try it out as you plan for teaching or microteaching. Revise the format as you see the need.*

Directions: Follow the guidelines below as you plan a problem-based lesson.

Planning Tasks

Content that is focus of lesson _____

_____

Lesson objectives
Content objective _____

_____

Investigation objectives _____

_____

Problem situation
Statement of problem if teacher-designed _____

_____

_____

_____

General domain if student-designed _____

_____

_____

_____

Composition of study teams
Number and size of groups _____

_____

_____

_____

Criteria for membership _____

_____

_____

_____

---

*A more elaborate planning activity for problem-based learning is available on the *Interactive Student CD-ROM.*

Materials and logistics requirements
  Materials needed _____

  Supplies and equipment needed _____

  People to contact _____

Conducting the lesson
  Procedures for orienting students to the problem _____
  _____
  _____

  Procedures for organizing students in study teams _____
  _____
  _____

  Notes/hints to remember as students work _____
  _____
  _____

  Important dates to remember _____
  _____

  Gantt chart of dates and activities _____
  _____

  Procedures for presentation of artifacts and exhibits _____
  _____
  _____
  _____
  _____

  Pitfalls to avoid _____
  _____
  _____
  _____

Activity 11.3: Observing Problem-Based Learning in Microteaching or Classrooms

Purpose: This form highlights key aspects of a problem-based learning lesson. It can be used to observe a peer in a microteaching laboratory or an experienced classroom teacher. It can also be used to assess a lesson you have taught and videotaped.

Directions: As you observe the lesson, check the category you believe describes the level of performance of the teacher you are observing. Also answer the general questions about the lesson at the bottom of the form. Because most problem-based lessons take several days or weeks to complete, it may take several days to complete this form.

Teacher Behavior	Level of Performance			
	Excellent	Acceptable	Needs Improvement	Not Needed
Planning:				
How appropriate was the lesson's content?	_____	_____	_____	_____
How clear were the content objectives?	_____	_____	_____	_____
How clear were the investigative objectives?	_____	_____	_____	_____
How well did the problem situation meet criteria?	_____	_____	_____	_____
How well were study teams organized?	_____	_____	_____	_____
How appropriate and sufficient were materials and supplies to support lesson?	_____	_____	_____	_____
How well prepared was the teacher overall?	_____	_____	_____	_____
Execution:				
How well did the teacher:				
Explain purposes and goals?	_____	_____	_____	_____
Orient students to problem situation?	_____	_____	_____	_____
Organize students in study teams?	_____	_____	_____	_____
Assist students in study teams?	_____	_____	_____	_____
How well did the teacher:				
Explain expectations for presentations/artifacts/exhibits?	_____	_____	_____	_____
Organize presentations or exhibits?	_____	_____	_____	_____
Recognize individual effort?	_____	_____	_____	_____
Recognize team effort?	_____	_____	_____	_____

Overall Planning

What did you like best about the way the lesson was planned and organized?

_____

_____

What could be improved?

_____

_____

Lesson Execution

What did you like best about the way the lesson was conducted?

_____

_____

What could be improved?

_____

_____

Activity 11.4: Interviewing Teachers about Their Use of Problem-Based Learning

Purpose: For many years, educators have promoted and fostered inquiry and discovery approaches to learning. Since Dewey's time, teachers have been admonished to spend less time teaching low-level basic information to students and more time developing critical thinking skills and helping students construct their own knowledge. Some observers do not believe much progress has been made over the years. This activity will give you an opportunity to investigate beliefs held by experienced teachers about inquiry-oriented, problem-based instruction.

Directions: Use the questions below as a guide for interviewing teachers about their use or non-use of problem-based learning.

1. In what situations in your teaching do you use teaching methods that might be classified as inquiry-oriented teaching or problem-based instruction?

2. What do you see as the major strengths of this type of teaching?

3. What do you see as the major drawbacks of this type of teaching?

4. Some people believe that American schools spend too much time teaching basic information and not enough time promoting higher-level thinking and problem solving. What do you think?

5. If you want to spend more time on problem-based learning in your classroom, are there barriers that prevent you from doing so? If so, what are they?

Activity 11.5: Portfolio: Designing and Illustrating Problem Situations

Purpose: Thinking up unique and interesting topics and situations for problem-based lessons is among the most difficult aspects of this model. The purpose of this portfolio activity is to help you gain skill in designing problem situations and to develop products of your work that can become part of your teaching portfolio.

Directions: Follow the steps here to design two problem situations and to display them in words and pictures in your portfolio.

STEP 1: Choose two topical areas from one of your teaching fields for which you might someday use problem-based instruction. Choose one of these areas because it would lend itself to a few days of instruction. Choose the other because it would take several weeks to complete a problem-based lesson.

STEP 2: Make problem situations out of both topics and draw a web (see Chapter 9) showing how the problem situation can be divided into sub-topics. Put the sub-topics in some logical order, showing how they relate to one another. Use the criteria provided in this chapter to guide your problem selection.

STEP 3: Make a plan showing how you would visually illustrate and introduce the two problem situations. For one of the situations, assume that you are defining the problem for students. For the other, assume that you are helping students define the problem for themselves within the broad confines of your school curriculum.

STEP 4: Critique your work with a reflective essay. How appropriate were the problem situations you selected? What kinds of problems did you face in planning your introduction?

STEP 5: Arrange the following in your portfolio: the two problem situations, your introduction of them, pictures illustrating the problems for students, your web showing relationships among the sub-topics, and your reflective essay.

CHAPTER 12

CLASSROOM DISCUSSION

Activity 12.1   Assessing My Discussion and Discourse Skills
Activity 12.2   Observing Discussion in Microteaching or Classrooms
Activity 12.3   Observing Student Participation in Discussion
Activity 12.4   Observing Teacher Use of Questions and Wait-Time
Activity 12.5   Portfolio: Demonstrating Your Executive Control of Questioning

Activity 12.1: Assessing My Discussion and Discourse Skills

Purpose: Use the chart below to assess your level of skill in building productive discourse systems and conducting effective discussions.

Directions: Check the level of skill you think you have for the areas listed below.

Understanding or Skill	Level of Understanding or Skill		
	High	Medium	Low
Planning tasks:			
Considering purposes for discussions	_____	_____	_____
Considering student skill prior to discussions	_____	_____	_____
Making plans for discussions	_____	_____	_____
Interactive tasks:			
Focusing discussions	_____	_____	_____
Keeping discussions focused	_____	_____	_____
Keeping records of discussions	_____	_____	_____
Listening to student ideas	_____	_____	_____
Using wait-time	_____	_____	_____
Responding to students' answers	_____	_____	_____
Responding to students' ideas	_____	_____	_____
Closing and debriefing discussions	_____	_____	_____
Evaluation and assessment:			
Making plans for follow-up	_____	_____	_____
Grading	_____	_____	_____
Helping students become more effective in discourse systems:			
Slowing down the pace	_____	_____	_____
Broadening participation	_____	_____	_____

Activity 12.2: Observing Discussion in Microteaching or Classrooms

Purpose: This form highlights key aspects of a classroom discussion lesson. It can be used to observe a peer in a microteaching laboratory or an experienced classroom teacher. It can also be used to assess a lesson you have taught and videotaped.

Directions: As you observe the lesson, check the category you believe describes the level of performance of the teacher you are observing. Also answer the general questions about the lesson at the bottom of the form.

Teacher Behavior	Level of Performance			
	Excellent	Acceptable	Needs Improvement	Not Needed
Planning:				
How appropriate was the discussion's focus?	_____	_____	_____	_____
How clear were the content objectives?	_____	_____	_____	_____
How clear were the discourse objectives?	_____	_____	_____	_____
How appropriate was the type of discussion?	_____	_____	_____	_____
How appropriate was the way the teacher used the physical space?	_____	_____	_____	_____
How well prepared was the teacher overall?	_____	_____	_____	_____
Execution:				
How well did the teacher:				
Explain purposes and goals?	_____	_____	_____	_____
Orient students to the discussion?	_____	_____	_____	_____
Keep the discussion focused?	_____	_____	_____	_____
Use methods to record the discussion?	_____	_____	_____	_____
Encourage broad participation?	_____	_____	_____	_____
Use wait-time?	_____	_____	_____	_____
How well did the teacher:				
Bring the discussion to a close?	_____	_____	_____	_____
Debrief the discussion?	_____	_____	_____	_____

Overall planning

What did you like best about the way the lesson was planned and organized?

_____

_____

What could be improved? _____

_____

_____

Lesson execution

What did you like best about the way the lesson was conducted?

_____

_____

What could be improved? _____

_____

_____

Activity 12.3: Observing Student Participation in Discussion

Purpose: Broad student participation is an important goal in classroom discussions. This activity can be used to gather information about patterns of student participation in class discussions.

Directions: Obtain a copy of the class seating chart or, if observing a small group, note everyone's name and location on your paper. You can use a format like the one pictured here. Whenever a student contributes to the discussion, make a "tick" on your chart by that student's name.

		Front		
❑_____	❑_____	❑_____	❑_____
❑_____	❑_____	❑_____	❑_____
❑_____	❑_____	❑_____	❑_____
❑_____	❑_____	❑_____	❑_____

Analysis and Reflection: Who talks the most? The least? Is there an action zone, that is, an area of the room that the teacher seems to favor during whole-class discussions? Are there any sex differences in participation? Racial differences? Any other patterns observed? How might the quieter students be encouraged to participate?

Activity 12.4: Observing Teacher Use of Questions and Wait-Time

Purpose: In order to extend and strengthen student thinking, teachers need to have good questioning skills. This activity is to help you analyze teachers' use of questions, such as number of questions asked, cognitive level of questions, and wait-time.

Directions: There is a column labeled *Code,* another labeled *Question No.,* and other columns labeled *A, B, C,* and *D.* The *Code* column is your key for determining what code goes in each column. For the first question the teacher asks, go to the *Question No.* column and find *1.* Then read across to column *A* and code in that column the level of question that the teacher asked—a knowledge question would be coded *1,* an application question *3,* and so on. Then code in column *B* for question *1* the appropriate wait-time code. Follow the same procedure for columns *C* and *D,* and repeat the procedure for each question the teacher asks.

Code	Question No.	A	B	C	D
A. Level of question					
1. Knowledge	1	—	—	—	—
Can the students recall what	2	—	—	—	—
they have seen, heard, or read?	3	—	—	—	—
For example, what is the					
meaning of *longitude?*					
2. Comprehension	4	—	—	—	—
Can the student organize facts	5	—	—	—	—
in various ways? For example,	6	—	—	—	—
what is the main idea in					
this paragraph?					
3. Application	7	—	—	—	—
Can the student apply techniques	8	—	—	—	—
and rules to solve problems that	9	—	—	—	—
have single correct answers? For					
example, if Bill has 49 cents, how					
many 8-cent balloons can he buy?					
4. Analysis	10	—	—	—	—
Can the student explain relationships,	11	—	—	—	—
make inferences, and find examples to	12	—	—	—	—
support generalizations? For example,					
religion was the focal point of life in					
the Middle Ages. What have you read					
that supports this idea?					

Code	Question No.	A	B	C	D
5. Synthesis	13	—	—	—	—
Can the student make predictions, solve problems, or produce original communications? For example, if school were not required, what would happen?	14	—	—	—	—
	15	—	—	—	—
6. Evaluation					
Can the student give opinions about issues and judge the merit of ideas, problem solutions, art, and other products? For example, do you agree that honesty is always the best policy?	16	—	—	—	—
	17	—	—	—	—
	18	—	—	—	—
7. Rephrasing the previous question, cueing.	19	—	—	—	—
	20	—	—	—	—

B. Wait-time

    1. Teacher paused a few seconds *before* calling on student.

    2. Teacher paused a few seconds *after* calling on student.

    3. Teacher did not pause.

    4. Not applicable; student answered readily.

C. Level of difficulty

    1. Student response was accepted by teacher.

    2. Response was not accepted by teacher.

D. Teacher response to student answers

    1. Teacher gave a brief acknowledgment of correct answer.

    2. Teacher gave gushy praise.

    3. Student error was "dignified."

    4. Student error was handled inappropriately.

Comments:

_____

_____

_____

_____

Activity 12.5: Portfolio: Demonstrating Your Executive Control of Questioning

Purpose: To help you gain skill in questioning and to develop understanding of the effects of various questions. The result can become a work product for your portfolio.

Directions: Following the steps here, develop a list of questions that might be asked in a discussion, try them out with an audience, and visually document this work for your portfolio.

STEP 1:   Choose a topic in your teaching field and develop a list of questions that might be asked in a discussion. Have at least one question from each of the six cognitive processes in Bloom's Revised Taxonomy. Use Table 12.3 on page 435 as a guide in developing the different types of questions.

STEP 2:   Find a small group of three or four students, friends, or family who would be willing to have you question them in a discussion-type format, and have this activity videotaped.

STEP 3:   Ask the group each of your prepared questions, and record their responses.

STEP 4:   Review your video recording and analyze the responses elicited by the various levels of questions.

STEP 5:   Write a critique of your questioning. Did it go as you planned? How did responses differ according to the type of question asked?

STEP 6:   Arrange the following in your portfolio: your questions, your video, and your critique.

CHAPTER 13

SCHOOL LEADERSHIP AND COLLABORATION

Activity 13.1   Assessing My Workplace Skills
Activity 13.2   Diagnosing the School's Ability to Meet Personal Needs
Activity 13.3   Interviewing Teachers about Role Conflict
Activity 13.4   Interviewing Teachers about Involving Parents
Activity 13.5   Portfolio: My Platform on Effective Schooling

Activity 13.1: Assessing My Workplace Skills

Purpose: Norms in schools, as in any organization, are powerful forces that shape teacher, administrator, student, and even parent behavior. It is possible for teachers to influence these norms in a positive way. Using this tool, you have the opportunity to assess what you consider your level of effectiveness might be in helping develop positive norms of collegiality.

Directions: Mark the response that you think reflects what your level of skill or understanding would be in each area. If you discover that you feel a weakness in any, discuss with other students or practicing teachers how it might be overcome.

Understanding or Skill	Level of Understanding or Skill		
	High	Medium	Low
Developing collegiality in my work with colleagues			
Observing teachers	_____	_____	_____
Discussing educational issues	_____	_____	_____
Working in small groups	_____	_____	_____
Developing collegiality in my work with administrators			
Meeting with principal	_____	_____	_____
Informing principal of classroom activities	_____	_____	_____
Inviting principal to observe my class	_____	_____	_____
Writing complimentary notes to principal	_____	_____	_____
Seeking out support from other school and district leaders	_____	_____	_____
Developing collegiality in my work with parents			
Reporting classroom activities to them	_____	_____	_____
Holding conferences	_____	_____	_____

Activity 13.2: Diagnosing the School's Ability to Meet Personal Needs

Purpose: The purpose of this activity is to help you assess organizational understanding. It is intended to increase your ability to see the ways schools operate to help or hinder their members in meeting their needs for achievement, affiliation, and influence.

Directions: Use the questions below to interview teachers or administrators about their schools. Be sure to probe for specific examples.

School Interview Schedule

Our _____ class has been studying some aspects of organizational psychology. We have been learning about how organizations can serve as vehicles to satisfy such basic human needs as:

1. *Affiliation:* The need for friendship, for working with others, for warmth and caring.

2. *Influence:* The need for power, for having control over one's life and one's destiny.

3. *Achievement:* The need to experience success, to do well in work, to find new and better ways of doing things.

We are trying to find out how this school offers its staff and students opportunities for friendship, influence, and success. We appreciate your willingness to give us your views on this topic.

Let's start with some questions about you and the way you experience the school as a (principal, vice-principal, teacher).

1. Over what aspects of your work do you feel most influential? (Probe to get the person to list specific tasks such as, "I feel I have a great deal of influence when I make out the daily schedule and when I determine which textbook to use in my class.")

   a. _____

   b. _____

   c. _____

   d. _____

2. Over what aspects do you feel least influential?

   a. _____

   b. _____

   c. _____

   d. _____

3. Can you name two or three things (pertaining to work here at school) that you have done in the past year that gave you a real sense of accomplishment?

   a. _____

   b. _____

   c. _____

   d. _____

4. What happens here at school that makes you feel close and warm toward others or that enables you to experience feelings of closeness and warmth from others?

   _____

   _____

   _____

   Now let's turn to the school in relation to experiences provided for students.

5. From your viewpoint, which experiences provided here at _____ give students the best chance to feel influential?

   a. _____

   b. _____

   c. _____

   d. _____

6. From your viewpoint, is _____ a place where students have a lot of friends and like being involved with others? (If yes, ask for examples; if no, probe for reasons.)

_____

_____

_____

7. From your viewpoint, is _____ a place where most students take pride in their work and strive to do well? (If yes, ask for examples; if no, probe for reasons.)

_____

_____

_____

_____

8. What ideas or suggestions do you have that could make _____ a place where students would experience more friendship, greater influence, and more success?

_____

_____

_____

Analysis and Reflection: Write a paragraph responding to the following questions: What are your reactions to the activities teachers mentioned as contributing to their influence, achievement, and affiliation needs? Would these kinds of activities satisfy you? Why or why not?

Activity 13.3: Interviewing Teachers about Role Conflict

Purpose: Teachers work with many role expectations, some of which are clear and straightforward, and some of which conflict with each other. Teachers wrestle with how to resolve conflicting role expectations and arrive at different strategies for accomplishing it. Use this activity to give you some ideas about how you might achieve your own resolution of role conflict by discovering how other teachers have achieved it.

Directions: Use the following questions to guide you in interviewing one or two teachers about role conflict.

1. Do you value treating students as individuals?
2. What do you do to show students that you value them as individuals and are attempting to tailor instruction to their needs?
3. How many students do you teach every day? Do you teach mostly to groups of students or individuals?
4. How do you resolve the dilemma between treating students as individuals and teaching that many students every day?
5. Do you think it is important to be on close terms with students in order to better teach them?
6. Do you think it is important to maintain some social distance from students in order to maintain discipline?
7. How do you resolve the dilemma between fostering closeness with students for teaching purposes and yet maintaining distance for discipline purposes?

Analysis and Reflection: Using these teachers' responses as a jumping-off place, write a paragraph about how you might initially try to deal with resolving these conflicting role expectations for yourself.

Activity 13.4: Interviewing Teachers about Involving Parents

Purpose: Establishing good working partnerships with parents is very important. One way this can be done is by using parents as helpers in the classroom. The purposes of this activity are twofold: to help you develop an awareness of the things parents can do and to alert you to how you can plan to make parent helping go smoothly.

Directions: Use these questions as a guide in talking with teachers about using parents as helpers.

1. In what ways do you use parents as helpers?
   ___ In class, conducting small groups
   ___ As assistants for field trips
   ___ As assistants for special events in school
   ___ As teacher aides (correcting papers, putting out newsletter, and so on)
   ___ At home, helping with homework
   ___ Other *(Specify)*_____

   _____

2. How did you locate parents for these tasks?

   _____

   _____

   _____

   _____

3. Was it necessary to train parents for these tasks? If so, what did the training consist of? Who conducted the training? How long did it last?

   _____

   _____

   _____

4. What sorts of problems have you run into in using parents? How have you solved these problems?

   _____

   _____

5. How have you provided recognition to parents for their efforts?

   _____

   _____

   _____

6. What benefits have accrued to you, to parents, and to students as a result of using parents as helpers?

   Benefits for teacher: _____

   _____

   _____

   Benefits for parents: _____

   _____

   _____

   Benefits for students: _____

   _____

   _____

Analysis and Reflection: Consider your own subject area or grade level. In light of what this teacher has told you about using parents for helpers, how might you utilize parent help? What kind of training will parents need? How will you arrange for parent training? How will you arrange for parent recognition? Write a paragraph in response to these questions.

Activity 13.5: Portfolio: My Platform on Effective Schooling

Purpose: At the end of Chapter 1, you were asked to prepare a *platform* with several *planks* that expressed your thinking at that time about teaching and learning. Remember that we described the platform as your overall conception of teaching and learning, and the planks as your more specific beliefs and values. The purpose of this exercise is to have you extend your platform, taking into account the content of this chapter on teachers' work and aspects of effective schooling.

Directions: Create a platform on teachers' work and on effective schools by doing the following:

STEP 1:   Add two or three pages to the platform you wrote in Chapter 1 that describe your current beliefs about the organizational functions of teaching, the features of effective schools, and the implications this has for your work as a teacher. Your platform should be supported by clear and specific planks that include your beliefs and values in regard to effective schools, research, research on teachers' work, and the professional community.

STEP 2:   Include in your discussion the various features of effective schools that were illustrated in the text, and write how much you agree or disagree with the various features based on your own work or observations in schools.

STEP 3:   Discuss the organizational aspects of teaching, and consider which aspect of teachers' work you value the most and which aspects you will find most troublesome. For example, do you look forward to working with colleagues and parents, or do you see this aspect of what teachers do as taking valuable time away from your work with students?

STEP 4:   You may wish to illustrate your platform with photographs of schools, videos, papers, and other artifacts that will demonstrate to others your understanding of the school as places where teachers work and of the features that make some schools more effective than others.

NOTES

NOTES

NOTES

NOTES

NOTES

NOTES

NOTES

NOTES

NOTES

NOTES

NOTES

NOTES

NOTES

NOTES